Bernadette of Lourdes

Greg

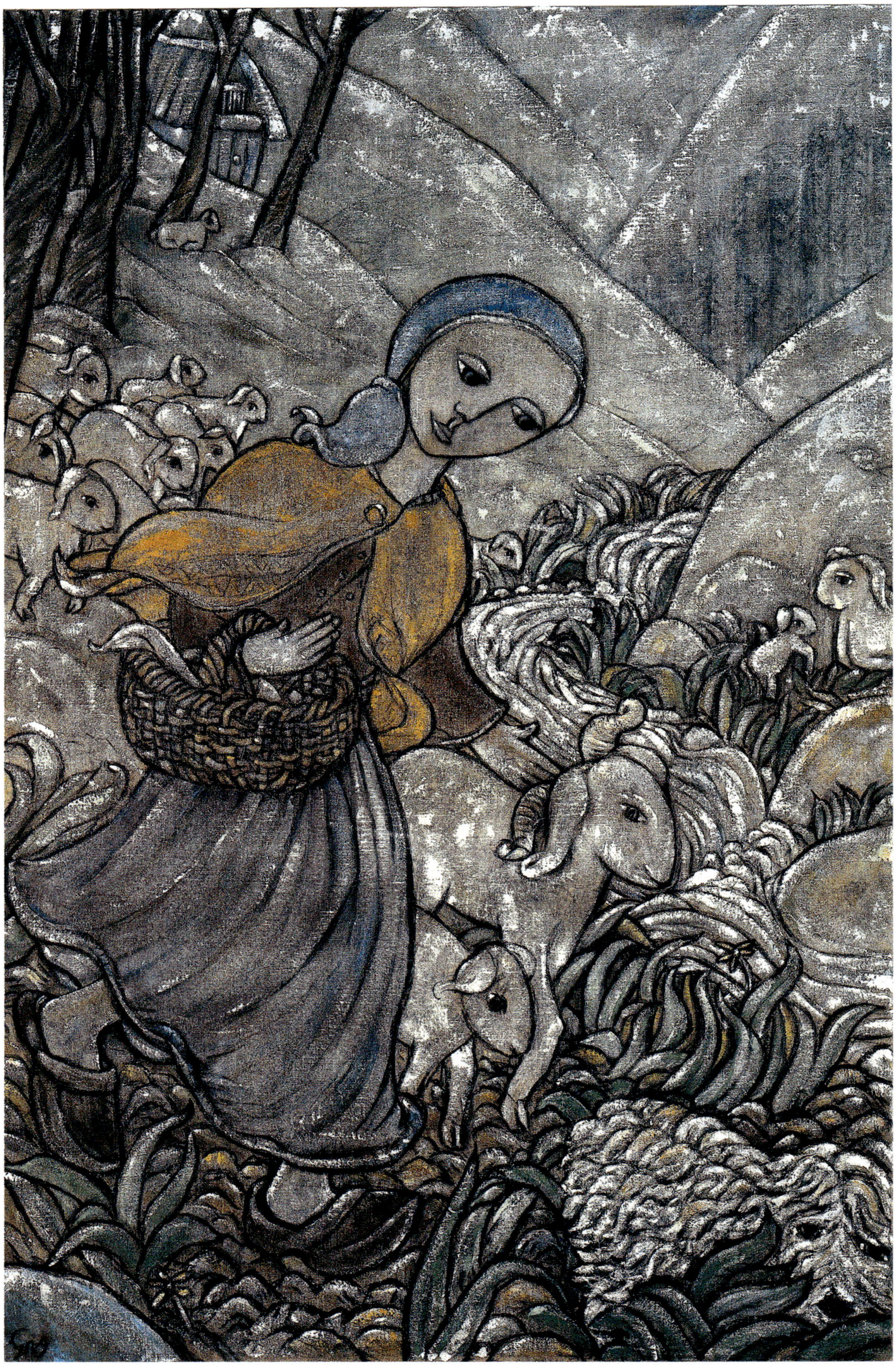

Bernadette of Lourdes

THE MYSTERY OF MARY & THE ETERNAL FEMININE

Paintings & Sculptures

by GREG TRICKER

Foreword by

SISTER WENDY BECKETT

Essay by

PHILIP VANN

PAUL HOLBERTON PUBLISHING
LONDON

The St Bernadette Paintings exhibited at the Piano Nobile Gallery,
London 2008, with the accompanying book, mark the
150th Anniversary of St Bernadette's
visitations at Lourdes in
1858

BERNADETTE OF LOURDES

THE MYSTERY OF MARY & THE ETERNAL FEMININE

Published and distributed by Paul Holberton Publishing in 2008
89 Borough High Street, London SE1 1NL
www.paul-holberton.net

Produced by Greg Tricker in association with Piano Nobile Gallery

Type setting and layout by Christopher Challen

The stories that complement each of the plates on pages 36–136
were collated by Greg Tricker, with reference to the original
source material as outlined in the bibliography.

ISBN 9781903470886

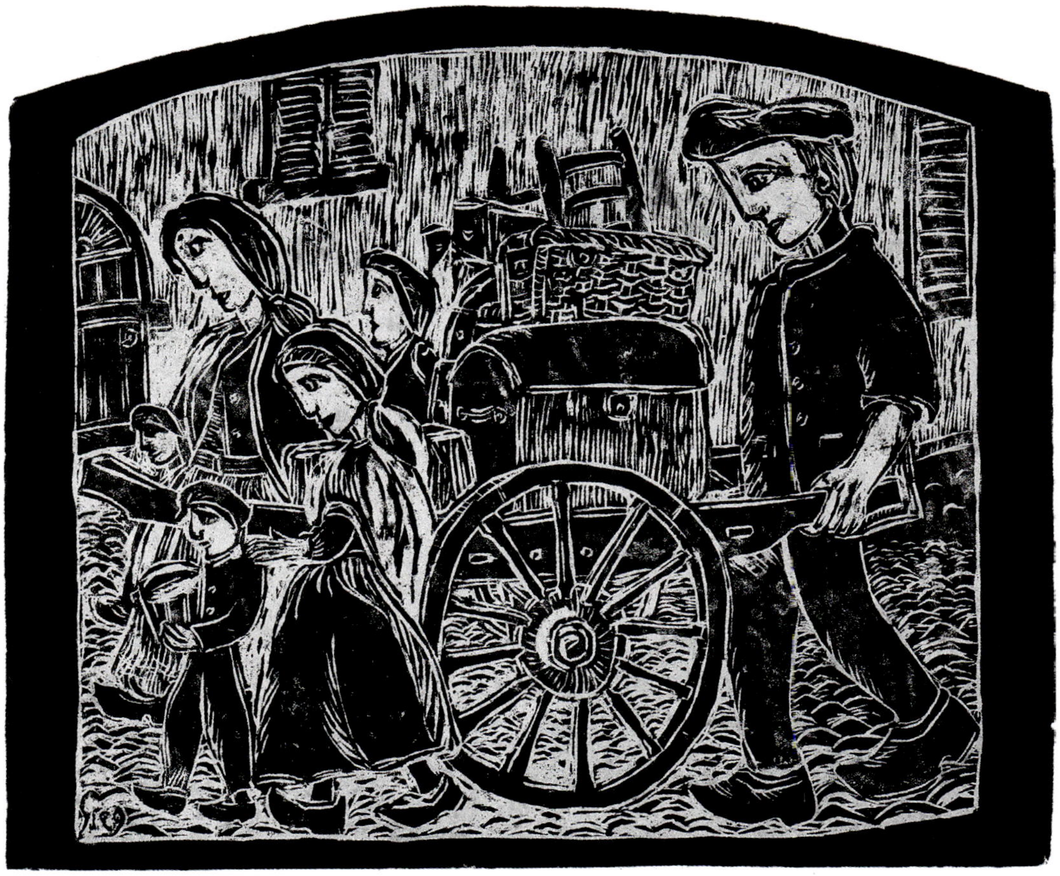

Greg Tricker's paintings and sculptures are represented by

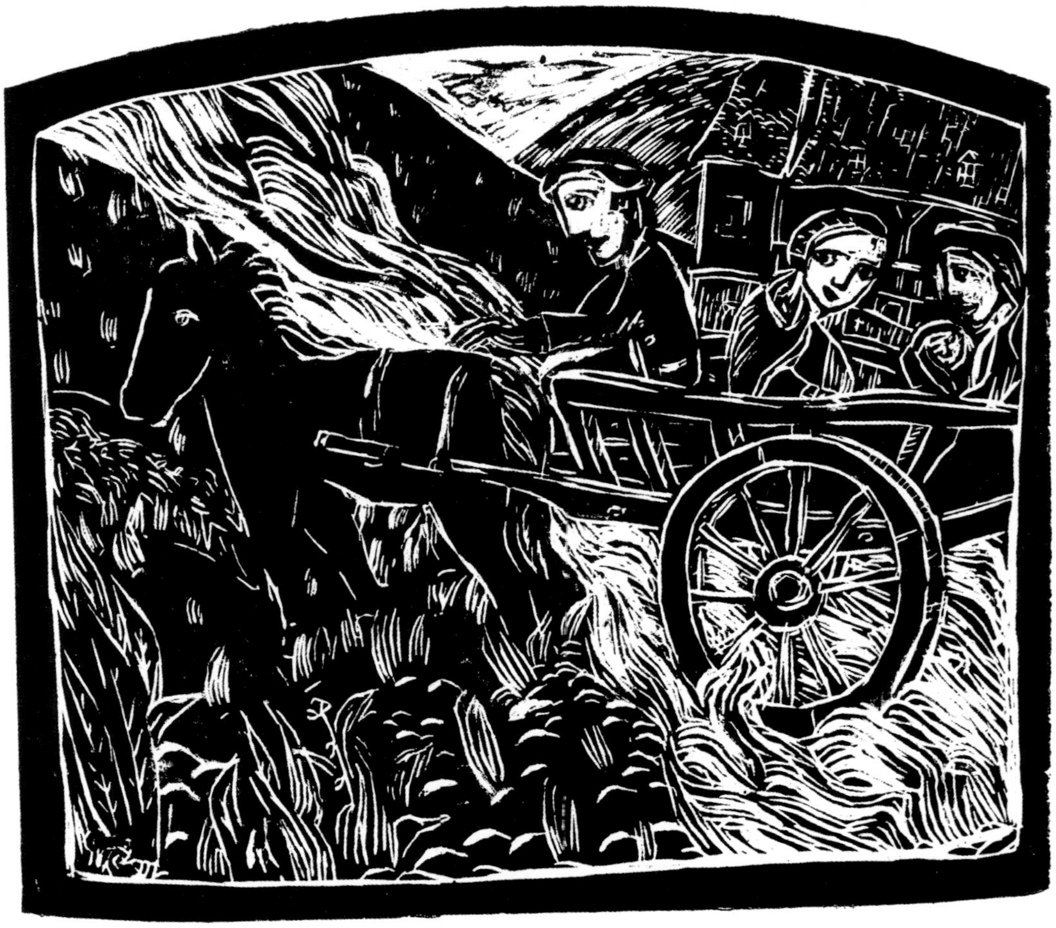

Contents

List of Plates

Foreword

by Sister Wendy Beckett

St Bernadette

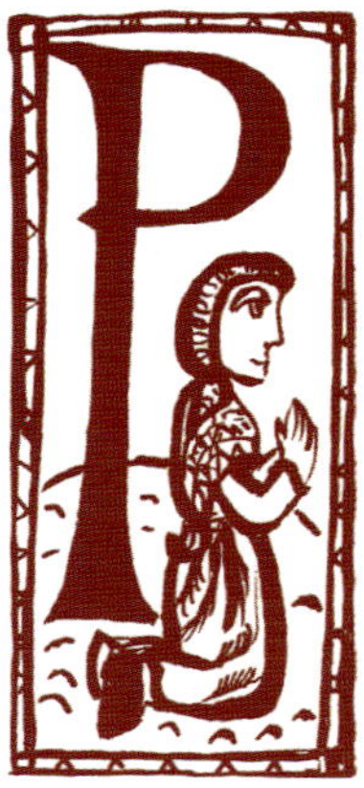

PERHAPS more than any other saint, St Bernadette Soubirous shows us what sanctity means. She was born in 1844, the oldest child of a peasant family from Lourdes, on the threshold of the Pyrenees, and she died in 1879. In those 35 years, her sole 'accomplishments' seem to have been that when she had barely turned fourteen, she saw the Blessed Virgin, and that then she became a nun. The apparitions came to her, they were a gift, and many Catholic girls of the nineteenth century became nuns. Yet Bernadette, desperately poor, uneducated, (she had hardly ever been to school), sickly and undernourished, accepted that gift so profoundly and so simply that it transformed her into holiness. Sanctity is God's gift, not our doing: St Bernadette makes this radiantly clear.

She was a deeply reticent saint, and her life story has almost no incident except that of her encounter with the Virgin. This makes her exceedingly difficult to portray. It seems to me that it is because Greg Tricker has himself an affinity with silence and simplicity, that he is able to enter into the spiritual reality of St Bernadette. She was not understood by her generation, and Tricker too, is like no other artist. In an age where irony, political relevance, complexity and grandiloquence are in favour, Tricker has an amazing innocence and passion that is strangely reminiscent of St Bernadette. Yet this innocence is at the opposite extreme of ignorance: he has extraordinary command of techniques, painting, drawing, printing, sculpting, all with the same concentrated yet gentle power. He is concerned with a meaning beyond the surface, and it is to this 'beyond' that his eyes, hand and heart are committed. He feels that his sense of the Sacred and Divine is reflected in the deep blue that appears throughout his work and "this sacred blue"—Prussian—French ultra marine—indigo—"and the glowing green and yellow too" have a relationship to the stained glass of Chartres Cathedral that he visited before beginning the work. Tricker sees his blues as "reaching into the very fibre of the hessian, the poor peasant people close to God." He feels his work "resonates" with the peasants of Millet, and the potato eaters of Van Gogh. The richness and mystic power he feels relates to Samuel Palmer and to Rouault. Yet, even when he abjures jewel-like colour for the absolute whiteness of his sculpture, there is still an inner radiance that speaks of the transcendent.

It is not surprising that Tricker feels a kinship with the composer John Tavener who says his music comes from "the Angel of Inspiration". Tricker believes in this Angel, and adds "it is important to me that the alignment to God is humbly waited for and acted on and worked with. From that source and not my own small self and will power alone" comes what is created. "I have a part to play but always and only with its true relationship with God."

I sometimes think that simply looking at Greg Tricker's work can bring us to a state of grace.

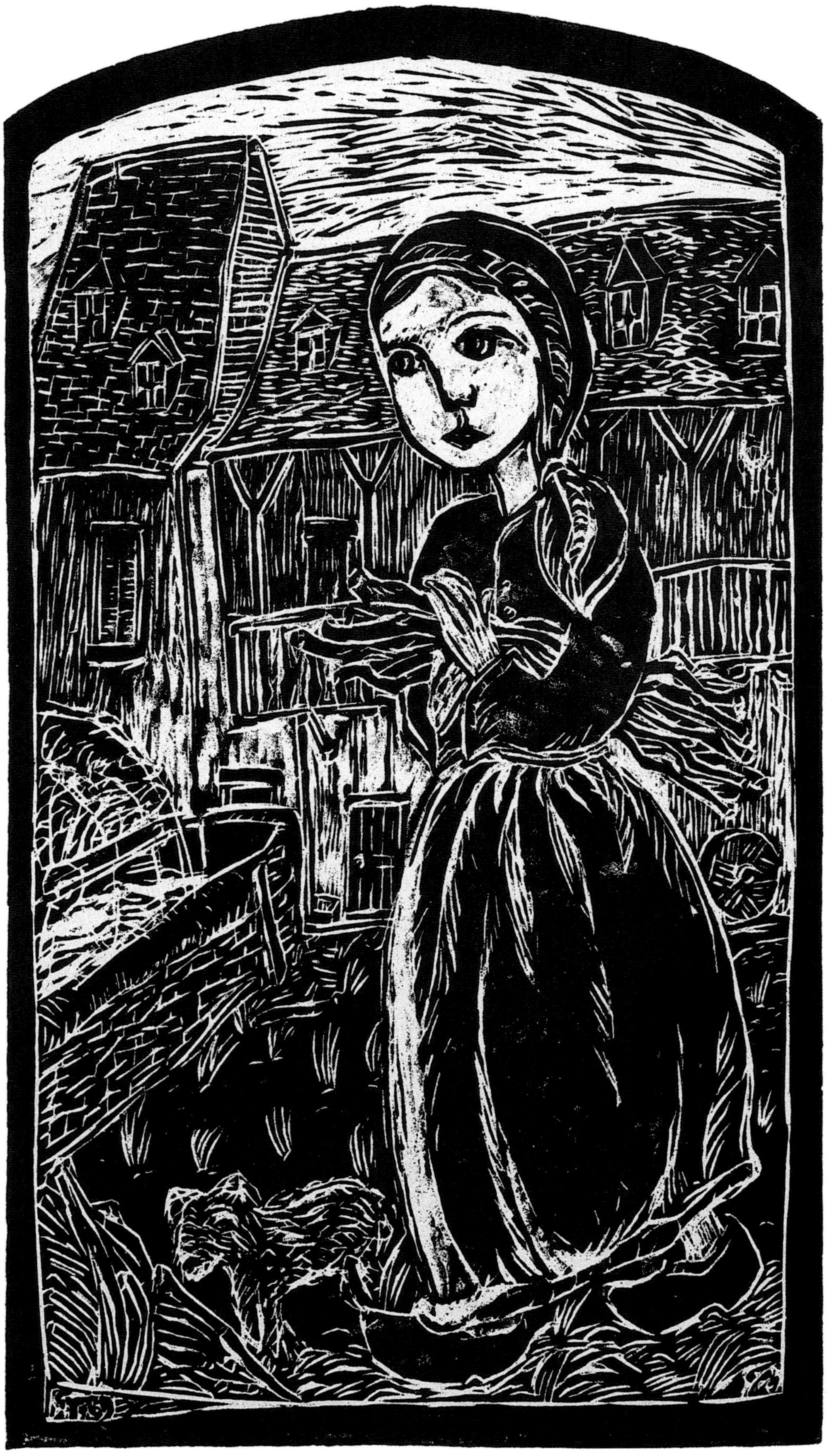

THE HEALING SPRING:
The Art of Greg Tricker and his Paintings & Sculptures of Bernadette of Lourdes

by Philip Vann

THE ART OF GREG TRICKER moves us with its subtle air of ardent simplicity, its heartfelt innocence and humane poignancy, qualities always allied to this artist's scrutinising intelligence and considerable painterly and sculptural sensitivity. He sees things as they are with a pristine urgency that strips away all mawkish, romanticising tendencies and easy conventionalities. That is why when he retells the stories in adventurous cycles, and related books, of sometimes up to sixty paintings, sculptures and woodcuts, he does so as an archetypal story-teller who literally re-searches his subjects with an empathetic understanding at once uncanny and astounding. The main cycles tell the stories of *Anne Frank* (for a book published in 1991), then of the early Christians living, worshipping and suffering in *The Catacombs* (2002), of *Francis of Assisi* (2005), of *Kaspar Hauser* (2006), the child imprisoned in early 19th century Nuremberg, and, now, Bernadette of Lourdes.

Though largely a self-taught artist, Greg is far from being a naïve one, though he does possess an unmistakeable, and indeed quite rare, childlike purity of vision, a sophisticated intuitiveness, of a kind that modern *avant-garde* artists have appreciated in the so-called naïve art of, say, Henri Rousseau, the Polish Nikifor, the Russian-Georgian Niko Pirosmani and Alfred Wallis. (In this context, we should recall the Latin roots of the word 'nativus', from which the term 'naïve' springs, meaning 'fresh, inborn, direct'). His wide-ranging cultural curiosity means that his art is nourished by gleanings from art he has long admired, ranging from medieval stained glass to the paintings of Millet, van Gogh, Rouault, Samuel Palmer, Chagall and Cecil Collins. But, as a true artist himself, he has, naturally enough, both overtly and unconsciously absorbed all kinds of influences and inspirations, artistic, religious and otherwise, into the humus of his craft, the crucible of his creativity. He escapes the pitfalls of merely illustrative or derivative narration, and invests his subject matter with a mystical authenticity that is (especially in the context of today's cynical cultural climate of tedious 'shock factors' and bare-faced nihilism) endlessly surprising and nourishing.

Greg Tricker was born in June 1951 in south London but the family moved to Bishop Stortford in Hertfordshire when he was three or four, so that they could be nearer to countryside. From his father, who was an architect who worked in London, Greg inherited what he calls 'a love of art and van Gogh in particular', and he was encouraged by him when he started painting quite intensively before the age of ten. 'My mother was very much a nature lover, who loved flowers, trees and walks. From her side, I had that very strongly.' As a young boy he felt increasingly alienated from his parents' fundamentalist Christianity, and his first prolific pictures (copying van Gogh's paintings and drawings)—which he now calls 'a workshop for me in colour, feeling and mood'—were an inexorable imaginative retreat for him. He says of that intense period of

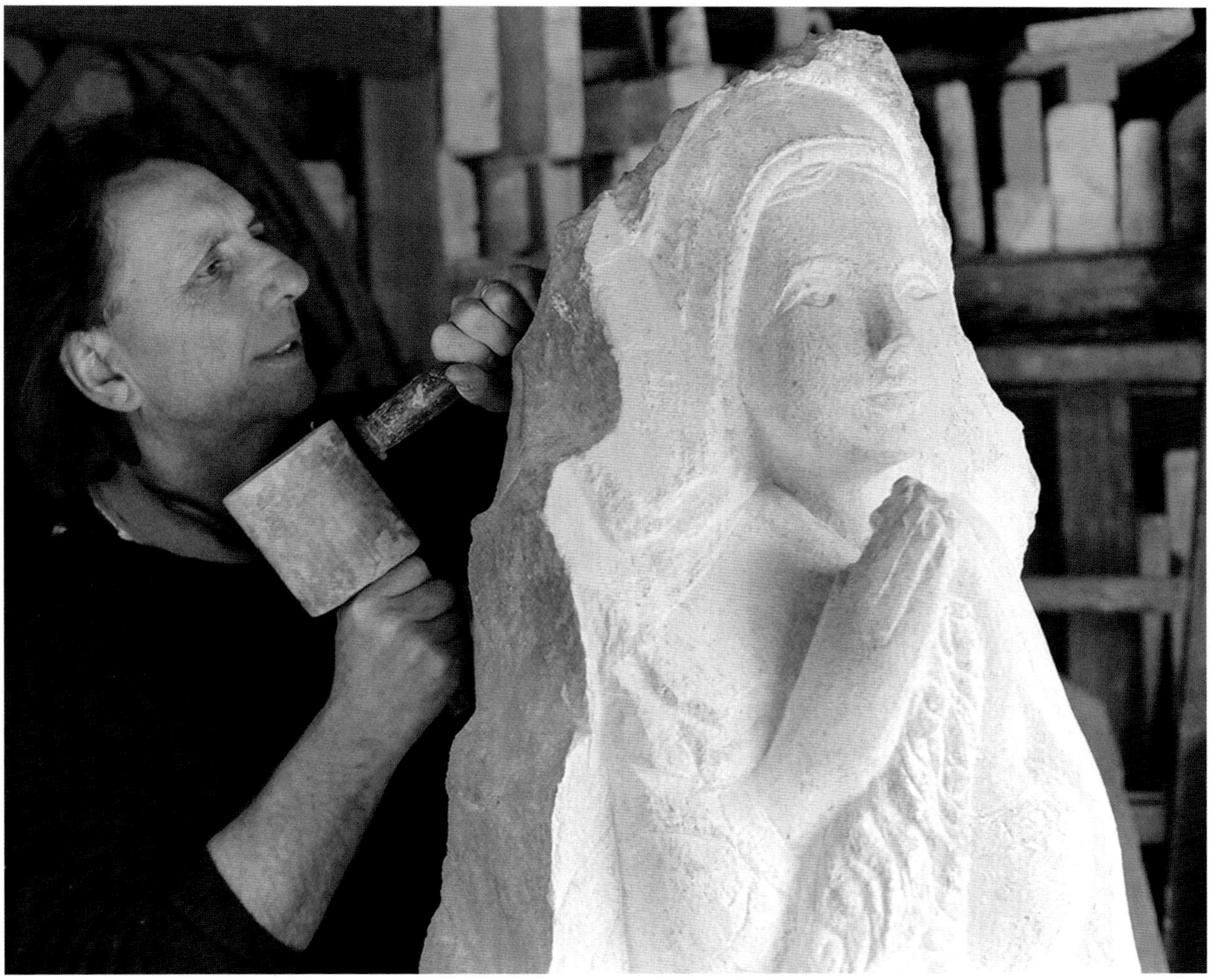

childhood and adolescence: 'I grew up with a feeling of my own inner isolation, and it linked with real art and colours imbued with pain and my own quest. I was also really sensing van Gogh's feelings.'

He left school at sixteen, and studied art and life drawing for a few months at Ware College in Hertfordshire. At this stage, he had given up any ideas about what he might do in life. However, he was introduced by a teacher there—Michael O'Connell, who had a studio on Henry Moore's estate—to the art of batik-painting, which proved inspiring. After a couple of years working in factories, Greg decided to hitch-hike to the Isles of Scilly. For six months initially, he worked as a hotel kitchen porter. Then he came back home for a time before returning to the island for, all in all, a few years. He was able to immerse himself in the beautiful daily surroundings, delivering milk for several months all over the island. He appreciated the Scilly Isles' atmosphere of rather archaic remoteness from the mainland, its close community spirit. 'It was fantastic being there. It opened up my mind. I was meeting a lot of young people. We were all knocking about together, doing jobs, working in hotels. And of course Bob Dylan was coming out then. There was a real "Times they are a-changing" feeling.'

ON the Scilly Isles, 'I was doing my batik work on the kitchen table.' He liked the subtle reverse, wax-resist process of batik-painting, which involves working in the negative whereby 'you're almost painting what you don't see – where the wax goes, the colour won't. It helped me, allowing me to channel in quite deep things, allowed them to appear backwards, as it were. I found a way in. That is what I did with the Anne Frank batik paintings, which I worked on later in 1987. After I'd worked in that way for a number of years, I was able to start painting directly onto canvas and wood. I was able to work forwards again.'

He met his first wife Carol on the Scilly Isles and they got married in Bristol in 1974, and settled in the village of Chew-stoke near Bath. He worked for a local stonemason repairing stones and cornices in houses sometimes in Bristol, and gradually started collecting odd pieces of stone to be used for carving. In September 1997, he moved to live and teach at Ruskin Mill College in Gloucestershire with his second wife Karin, and their son Joseph was born there two months later in their cottage overlooking the mill. He later qualified as a memorial mason and letter-cutter in stone, crafts he still continues to practise part-time. It is in his small, bare wooden studio (see page 142) on the wooded hills with a view of the mill and adjoining lake that he has painted his series of works based on the Catacombs, and on the lives of St Francis, Kaspar Hauser and St Bernadette.

Greg has never held back taking on subjects of immense, indeed almost inconceivable historical, religious and mythic importance. Yet his great gift is in making such stories humanely accessible, indeed wondrously simple, while retaining intimations of the vast mystery—and ultimately of the cosmic messages and reflections—underlying the seeming (and the actual) simplicity. He eschews the pretence of elaborately complex expression for its own sake, perhaps agreeing with the 18th century poet George Herbert:

> *There is in love a sweetness readie penn'd:*
> *Copie out onely that, and save expense.*

St Bernadette spoke in similar terms: 'The simpler one writes, the better it will be. In trying to dress things up, one only distorts them.'

Anne Frank Paintings

THE cycle of paintings *For Anne Frank* (see appendix[1] page 141) is dedicated by him 'To the innocent children who died'. He says, 'There's something so big in the subject of Anne Frank, and in the depth and destruction of the Holocaust, that I had to present the pictures in a very simple way, that was full of meaning.' Speaking of his paintings of Anne Frank, and also of certain pictures in other series like that of St Francis touching the leper or another of him communing with Brother Horse, he says 'there's something quite profound going on in the work, in a subtle, sensitive way: there's certainly a compassion behind the work.'

The pictures *For Anne Frank* work, remarkably, without a hint of bathos, false pathos or false rhetoric. We see Anne writing (see appendix[2]) on the pages of a book which themselves take on a feathery lightness, as if they are wings of dove-white incandescence winging away their message—one of anguished tenderness, of suffering through and enduring oppression, and the ultimate hope of real human understanding and tolerance—to the spirit of posterity. Anne's face, a ghostly green, in a snow-topped train hurtling under a black sky, tinged ominously with what may be green-tinged smoke, in the picture called *Loaded into cattle trucks*,[5] is an icon of human suffering and vulnerability at its most terrible. A final picture, entitled (in Anne's famous line) *I want to go on living even after my death*,[3] shows her, with an expression of heart-breaking wistfulness, cradling a dove above a heavenly white but still credibly human city. This dove of peace and transcendent serenity and hopefulness is resonant, in the viewer's mind, of the dove-like, feathery pages of Anne's diary we had seen earlier.

The apparently simplified colours and clothes and forms of *For Anne Frank* are perfectly in tune with those we intuit to have been those of late 1930s' and Occupied Continental Europe. Greg so immerses himself into each and every subject he portrays that he attains, in each case, an impressive degree of both atmospheric historical and geographical accuracy, and concomitant imaginative credibility too.

The paintings, sculptures and prints of *The Catacombs* also deal, like *For Anne Frank*, with people immured in darkness - their earthly fate, in this case, one of persecution at the hands of the Roman authorities, being sport for the lions at the Coliseum. In his researches, Greg visited Rome and what he calls 'the massive underground burial chambers of the early Christians'. He observed 'a painting of the Last Supper on a nearby wall. Although it was faded with age it was still possible to see the disciples gathering around the table with baskets of loaves.' Greg has made his own ethereally scumbled painting of this Last Supper, *Agape*,[8] in which haloed-Christ and his disciples in their simple pale blue skullcaps or *kippoth*, gather in gentle, compassionate amity before the fish and loaves and baskets (a moving parallel exists between this picture and the eerily monochrome one of a typically fearful supper of Anne Frank's family in the attic: *We sat around the table and waited*[4]). Though *The Catacombs* pictures refer to a persecuted religious minority, their atmosphere is one of joyful hope of a new life, a resurrection.[6] Greg himself has written that after seeing the Last Supper painting, 'From this dark tomb I emerged into the brilliant sunlight again, like Noah opening the door of the Ark.'[7] The lightness of touch and palette of this series, as well as its decorative peppering with ideogrammatic symbols found in the vaults, itself manages to resurrect a vital sense of an ancient culture in which a new radical Christianity fused in a transformative way with the mysteries, rites and sun-infused felicities and festivals of the wider, pagan Mediterranean world.

St Francis Paintings

THE pictures and sculptures of *Francis of Assisi* (tellingly subtitled *Paintings for our Time*) are more compositionally complex and exploratory than those in Greg's previous two series, though at their heart is a similar poignant simplicity. Greg was attracted to the subject of St Francis because 'he had this very inspiring dynamic—I think this was at the centre of the work for me —reaching across religion and laws. He seemed to bounce across. He seemed to say, what about the poor people? And then reach across to them or to the lepers. And it was also reaching Brother Sun[15] or Sister Moon. In a sense, the universe was brought closer, in a way almost as a family you could relate to. It's a feeling of all-embracing closeness.' This very feeling pervades Greg's portrayal of St Francis[9] inclining with sweet solicitude to fellow creatures (birds in the reed-beds, Brother Horse[11] or Sister Dragonfly); or one showing him reaching out with blissful intimacy to touch, in his simple sackcloth garments, some white flowers (snowdrops perhaps) blooming in an unpromising, frozen landscape beneath a blizzard, its impalpable contours conjured up with exquisite delicacy.[10]

There is a painting showing St Francis peering out from a grotto[12] (sited beneath a humble 12th century Mary chapel) where, Greg has written, 'he would stay in solitude. There is a small window here that overlooks the sheer drop of the ravine valley. When it was opened, St Francis could see the white doves flying in the early morning light, like Noah opening the latch of the Ark after a damp, dark journey of the soul.' The picture itself conjures up this scene with transcendent clarity. St Francis' countenance in profile itself seems tinged with the mossy green that suffuses the thick, dark stone grotto walls. He looks with gentle, open-mouthed awe at the window-framed scene of a dove flying against the steep hillside. The contrast between the heavily monumental, darkened interior and the fresh, fleeting, light aspect beyond is thrilling to contemplate. Some lines by W.H.Auden, from his 1939 poem *In Memory of W.B.Yeats*, spring to my mind here:

In the deserts of the heart
Let the healing fountain start,
In the prison of his days
Teach the free man to praise.

The existentialist nature underpinning Greg's highly diverse series of paintings is emphatically evident in this painting of St Francis gazing out of the *Carceri Hermitage*. Greg is attracted to the innate subversive radicalism of figures such as the early Christians, Anne Frank, St Francis, Kaspar Hauser[21] and St Bernadette. In different ways, each of them—confined within 'the prison of his [or her] days', stripped bare of egoistic preoccupations, most possessions, much of the outward paraphernalia of civilised living—discovers and celebrates an ineradicable inner freedom. Anne's message of essential universal humanity challenges all the discriminatory tribalisms of the wide world. St Francis upturned all contemporary religious notions as he, in Greg's words, 'trekked off with his Friars to Rome, bedraggled in all their rags, to see the Pope[13] on his throne, to seek sanction for his order. The story is that the Pope was baffled by it all, and that night had a dream about the Church falling down; there was this bedraggled friar trying to hold it up. So the Pope gave them his blessing, and they went back to Assisi, very happy.'

Kaspar Hauser Paintings

Greg's picture cycle, *Kaspar Hauser: The Holy Fool & The Path of Sacrifice* tells the famously enigmatic story of the young boy imprisoned for twelve years in a tiny, dark underground cell, near Nuremberg, with only his toy horse for company, then released in 1828 into a wider world which, by turns, bewilders and delights him, and one which, in the hands of an unknown assassin, finally destroys him. In his utterly untutored innocence, his blankness of experience, the mercilessly confined Kaspar experiences the world with an awe-inspiring openness. Greg depicts him drinking water from a little jug, his toy horse by his side, like a little sentient playmate. Kaspar had later written that he would take the jug to his mouth, not knowing 'that water had to be brought to me' nor that 'there could be anyone but me'. Greg calls this picture *The Water of Life*,[17] and it is striking that the bright water flows into his mouth on the side of his face which is shadowed black. After Kaspar's death, Greg celebrates the eternal spirit of the young man (and his eternally companionable toy horse) in a series of pictures of soaring cosmic redemption, in which Kaspar is seen variously as an *Ark Bearer*[19] like Noah, a Moses figure in the bulrushes ('as a saving seed; to raise mankind from captivity') and as a figure alongside Christ, moving together 'in the Ark Boat[20] across troubled waters, through the ages'. Ultimately, Kaspar is seen riding a celestial carriage with sun-like wheels, his resurrected toy horse beside him.[18] He has the cone-hatted appearance and demeanour of a Holy Fool, a longstanding archetypal figure in western culture about which Cecil Collins (in his 1944 text, *The Vision of the Fool*) wrote: 'The Fool represents that innate, inviolate, primordial innocence which...perceives directly or clearly...it seems to me that that is what life is about - the recovery of direct perception.'

These lines have their echo in the words of St Bernadette of Lourdes, referring to her mystical apparitions of the Virgin Mary in the grotto in Lourdes: 'How happy was my soul, Good Mother, when I had the good fortune to gaze upon you... Yes, you stooped down to earth to appear to a mere child... you deigned to make use of the most fragile thing in the world's eyes.'

St Bernadette

TAKING on the boundlessly deep subject of Bernadette for a new cycle of pictures and sculptures was another radical leap of faith for Greg. Just as previously he had 'felt drawn to Assisi and just had to go there', so researching the life of Bernadette he felt impelled to visit the places she had lived - her native town of Lourdes, nestling in the Pyrenees, nearby Bartrès (three miles away), on whose hillsides she had looked after sheep, and the distant Saint-Gildard convent at Nevers where she spent the latter part of her life. He recalls 'the start of it: going to Lourdes, I stood in this Basque kitchen at Boly Mill with a big fireplace across. She was born there in 1844, in one of the rooms. The water runs under the mill - all the grinding stones grind away.' The pictures of Bernadette's babyhood are ones of harmonious nurturing by parents and community, all redolent of a poor (but not as yet cruelly impoverished) peasant milieu. In *Mother and Father* (see page 39), we see her father François Soubirous (a surname meaning 'Sovereign'), the miller, and his wife Louise in their simple attire and sabots (clogs) looking down at the baby Bernadette in her fireside cradle. The mother's open book, the father's pipe and beret, their simple wooden, rush-seated chairs, the one candle on the fireplace, the crucifix hanging above, all indicate an atmosphere of happy, bare sufficiency, at a time when, albeit briefly, the family's worldly and spiritual needs were met.

The painting depicting the procession of 'happy local Bigourdans' making their way from Bernadette's christening down the snow-covered hill to Boly Mill (see page 41) to the sound of the imposing foreground accordion-player, is suffused with the music of maternal happiness, the bliss of babyhood. The contentment of her infancy, which helped give her an unswerving lifelong self-assurance, is evoked in the strong, dark, dignified forms in the painting *Mother and Child - Boly Mill* (see page 45), its fluid contours strikingly etched white. Early accidents in Bernadette's childhood were intimations of her own lifelong sufferings: her mother scalded herself when she was ten month's old and could not feed her for a while, so she was sent to a wet-nurse for a time at Bartrès, and her father lost an eye when it was cut while he was treating the surfaces of the millstones.

Bernadette was nearly two when she returned to Boly Mill from Bartrès. In *The Miller - Boly Mill* (see page 49), we see a fresh-faced Bernadette, doll in hands, looking up at her papa François, his face strongly tinged with green and blue, perhaps indicating a life of elemental experience and a knowledge of suffering, a bag of flour in his hands, the millwheel in the background. Greg has written of 'her merry sounds of words mingled with the splash and rumble of the revolving millwheel'. René Laurentin has noted that 'the most familiar noise to her in those first years was the sound of the millstones and the grain being ground. On her deathbed she would identify herself with the latter: "I have been ground in the mill like wheat."'

NATURE'S rich plenteousness at harvest-time is identified with human maternal intimacy and care in three mellifluous paintings recalling the occasion when Louise was working in the cornfields at a nearby farm and suddenly saw Bernadette carrying her younger brother Justin, seeking out her mother to feed the baby. In *The Golden Harvest* (see page 63), Bernadette strides with noble, upright composure between two sheaves of wheat, themselves like two golden pillars framing the figure perhaps evocative of Ceres, the ancient Roman goddess of the harvest and maternal love. In *Mother Harvest* (see page 59), Louise with baby Justin feeding at her breast and young Bernadette in her arm, recline in the semi-shade against sheaves of corn, a distant male figure seen loading bales onto carts. In this picture the golden, Samuel Palmer-esque or van-Gogh-like light of the harvest scene is imbued with more introspective blue tones, indicating notes of quiet human reflection and tender vulnerability. These paintings have an expansive timelessness about them too, recalling the mystical words of the 17th century poet Thomas Traherne: 'The corn was orient and immortal wheat, which never should be reaped nor was ever sown.'

The atmosphere of these pictures recalls too the paintings of Jean-François Millet, such as *The Gleaners* (1857) and *Summer: The Buckwheat Harvest* (1868–74), depictions of what feels like ceremonious peasant toil in the fields, and van Gogh's paintings (his own highly personal, sensuous versions of Millet's prints) of subjects such as *Peasant Woman Binding Wheat in Sheaves* and *The Sheaf-Binder* (both 1889). There is a resonance too of paintings like van Gogh's *Sower* (1888) and *Wheatfield with Reaper* (1889), the latter 'with a sun' which the artist said 'drenches everything in a golden light'. Greg acknowledges 'the link with the poor peasants in Millet's work, and then of course Millet's connection with van Gogh's work, *The Sower*, pictures of wheat fields and, of course, the poor *Potato Eaters*. It really struck a chord in my heart. It felt akin somehow. I realised how much I loved the peasant people, the poor millers. I think it was maybe the closeness they had to God as well, that they were simple people being near the sun and the earth. There was a certain closeness to the elements. That was one big factor drawing me

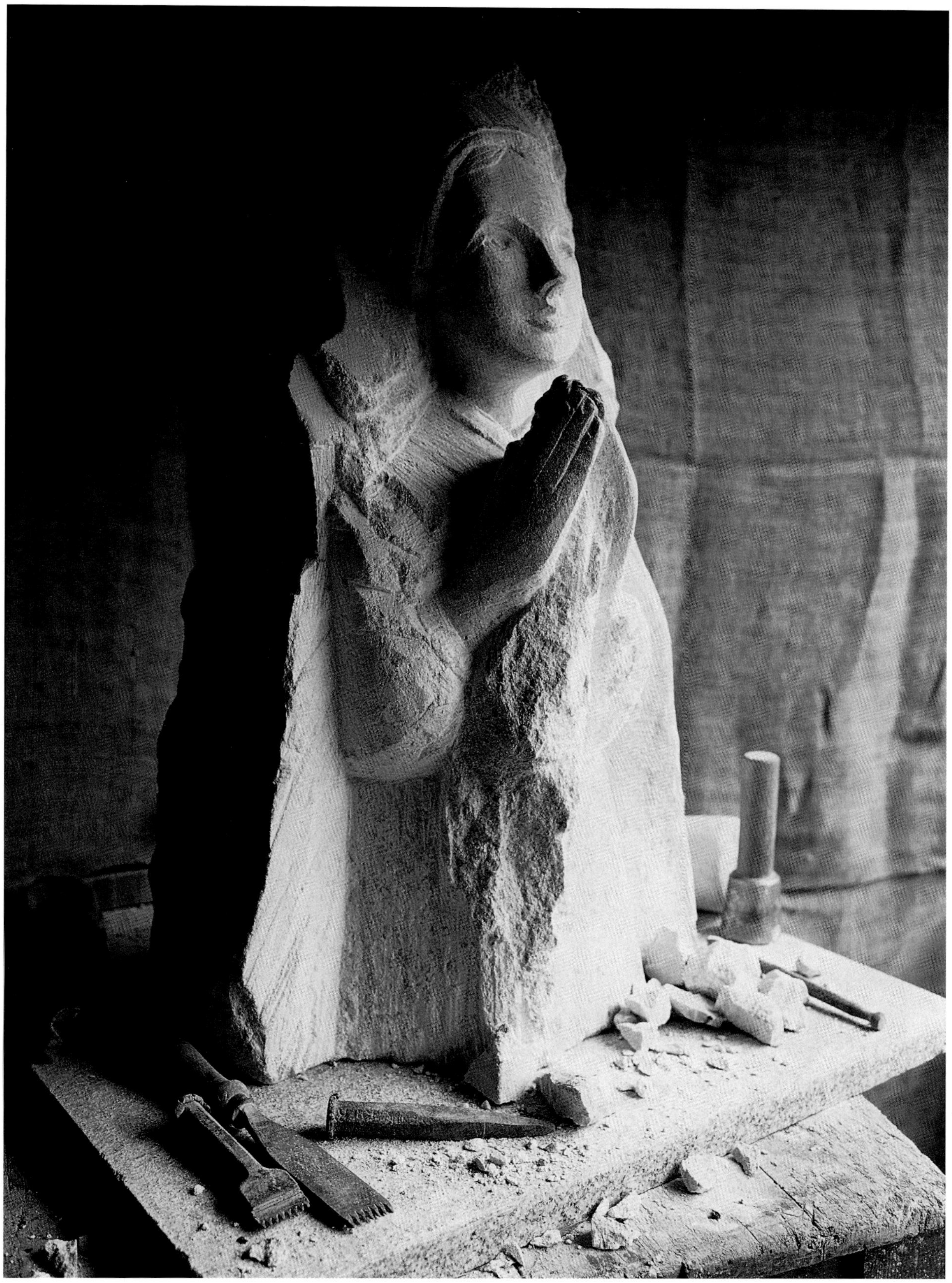

St Bernadette 34 x 21 x 12 inches, Farmington Limestone

in. It's almost like a stream running underneath the work, this feeling of van Gogh and Millet.'

This affinity Greg feels with the life the peasants led extends to his use of materials and frames here. 'The rough, hand-made oak frames I use here give a feeling of rough-hewn peasant life. I could easily plane them down, smooth them up, polish them but it would take away from the love I feel for a way of life. I generally seem to come across pieces of wood. Some of the wood I collect from a friend who cuts oak for planks, and I season them a while. The boards and canvases seem to come to me slowly, obliquely, and sometimes I see a piece of wood that has been discarded that I just love. It's like the surfaces talk to me.'

For his St Francis cycle of paintings, in the tempera and pencil picture of *St Francis with the Leper*,[14] Greg worked intimately and ingeniously with the grain and knottiness of the oak to evoke the leper's physical deformities - the sunken, misshapen area around his eye socket corresponding naturally to knots in the wood. So as St Francis is seen to caress the pitifully downcast leper with what feels like Christ-like compassion, we feel he is reaching out (almost across the universe, it seems) to a fellow human being whose misshapen mien—just like the unpredictable grain and warp of the wood itself—is an inescapable part of the natural scheme of things ultimately to be embraced wholeheartedly and without fear.

Returning to the Bernadette series, in *The Grinding Stones* (see page 53), we see François setting the powerful grinding stones in motion while Bernadette in her scarf and cape stands over the corn as it grinds down into pure white flour; the villagers wait at the door. The latter are being fed with a snack of fritters (often made by Bernadette with flour and oil) and cheese and (the then extremely precious gift of) wine by the couple; it was this kind of generosity towards his poor clients that contributed to the miller being made bankrupt and the family evicted from Boly Mill. The composition has a circular motion, extending from the central figure of François to that of his daughter, following a curve to the left as the corn is ground down, and culminating in the top left hand corner with the anticipatory peasants eating the (freely given) products of the Soubirous' labours. Bernadette's beatifically luminous look seems half abstracted, half concentrated on the brilliancy of the vessel of flour on the floor. Greg says of Bernadette, 'There was this interesting connection with the wheat; she did feel this grounding down. She said her life felt ground down like the corn. She had a very hard life; they were often living in damp and dismal conditions. She got asthma very young; she nearly died of cholera. There was a whole number of incidents that led to her being very weak, so she could hardly breathe quite often.' In *The Grinding Stones*, 'there's almost this pure white coming out of the flour; it's like making gold from base metal.'

In the woodcut *Bernadette Collects Firewood at Boly Mill* (see page 13), every detail—from the slates on the roof to the bundles of twigs in her arms, from the hairs on her pet dog Pigou's coat to the staves of the millwheel—is engraved with a deep attentiveness that mirrors the engaging concentration seen in Bernadette's demeanour and countenance. There is a raw meticulousness here which has echoes in medieval European woodblock prints.

In 1854, the family were turned out of Boly Mill, and moved to lodgings; François was forced to become a day labourer. Bernadette looked after her baby brother Justin, taking him to the fields, as we have seen, to be fed by his extremely hard-working mother. Laurentin has noted, 'Of the nine children that she eventually brought into the world, five did not survive to the age of ten.' The family went on to rent another mill but François had signed a ruinous contract. In 1857, they were forced to quit their seedy lodgings, and the only place they could find to live was Le Cachot, the small gaol room of the old prison, described at the time as a vermin-infested, 'foul, sombre hovel'.

Journey to Le Cachot (see page 69) shows the family trudging like refugees (which, in a deep sense, they were) on their way to the prison-house. This picture of peasant suffering has timeless resonances, relating to tragic human dispersals at all times in history. François trundles along, pushing the handcart stacked with their meagre belongings, his way made harder by the quite mountainous-seeming cobbles, on which we can almost sense the resounding clatter of all the heavy clogs. The two younger boys at the back of the procession seem oblivious of the situation, joking and having fun, whereas the parents and older children are burdened with sorrowful foreboding. Around them, subtly discernible are delicate, fluttering leaves, like little white feathers, evoking the family's predicament of being literally windswept as well as blown about by fate. The predominantly earthy brown palette here is suffused with blue tones 'in contrast', says Greg, 'with this really deep, dark feeling. The strength of the blues accentuates the nature of their poverty; the colour seems to highlight that. The sense of poverty mixed with this divine aspect, represented by the blues, is very strong.'

LIKE the painter Georges Rouault (1871–1958), in whom Greg feels 'this quiet sacredness, strength in the outline, the colours, the mood', and who had himself served an apprenticeship as a glass-maker, Greg increasingly finds himself identifying with the spiritually sturdy, anonymous artisans who built the medieval cathedrals, 'these poor people with their wheelbarrows, building stone by stone'. The radiant blues (suffusing the earthy browns) in Greg's pictures, have a subtly dynamic transporting power that recall for him the deep blues of stained glass at Chartres Cathedral, which he visited in the same year he went to Lourdes. 'Something in the sacredness in the blue at Chartres seems to penetrate into the pictures with Bernadette. I think it's also interesting that the origins of Chartres had this connection with Mary and the Black Madonna. There's a certain calm, a sacred feeling with blue, probably more than with any other colour. In these pictures, I've explored different blues, indigo, Prussian blue, a cerulean blue, a very light blue, and French ultra-marine.' The use of a range of blues is often especially apt in evoking compassion for 'poor, bare, forked' humanity (in Shakespeare's phrase), as Chagall demonstrated in a c.1915 gouache of a movingly gauche, blue-faced *Street Sweeper*, and Picasso supremely showed in his early figurative paintings made in Paris.

The heavy black outlines in some of Greg's picture seem also reminiscent of medieval stained glass, also to the pictures of certain modern artists, notably Rouault himself and Chagall. Greg says, 'Black and white are the foundation bones of the body, and colour seems to be the material, a way of feeling. Black on white is to me pure spirit, the essence of structure and existence. I have a deep reverence for colour. Colour is sacred. For example, I may link yellow with the sun, and to the wheat. To me, this becomes a living wheat intimately connected to St Bernadette's life at Boly Mill, the grinding stones and her feeling of being ground down like wheat'. He speaks of the painterly process: 'I feel inwardly drawn, a passion to work on a particular theme, even a particular piece of stone, wood or canvas. I sit in silence for a while, listening, looking into the grainy surface to feel out what is becoming present. I gently draw in lines with charcoal - the structure and the essence of the work. The colours flow around the structure, resonating together, imbued with my inner feelings, a sacred feeling, a feeling of reverence similar, maybe, to St Bernadette when she arranged flowers near the altar. Art is sacred work.'

In the curiously split composition of *Bernadette and the Stonemason* (see page 105), she looks beyond rough-hewn planks of the family's gaol room home into the workshop next door of a stonemason, André Sajous. From her perspective of dingy, earthly destitution, Bernadette appears on the threshold of a world of vibrant creativity, of ravishing Chartres-like reds, emerald greens, yellows and blues. It's as though, from her poverty-stricken perspective—the world of Emile Zola's scrupulously observed French working poor, the world of van Gogh's gnarled peasants having a sparse meal of potatoes and tea at a wooden-planked table—she yearningly glimpses a world of robustly defined colour, light and creative purpose. Greg says, 'it's as if she's looking into a world that's now disappeared, the world of hand-built crafts.' He links this world with the building of great cathedrals like Chartres, and says that this picture has 'almost a Resurrection feeling'. Yet paradoxically, it is noticeable that even Bernadette's poor, dark attire scintillates and glows from within, and the wooden planks of her claustrophobic home are burnished coppery and golden.

1857 and 1858 were years of widespread famine in rural France. In March 1857 François was falsely imprisoned for supposedly stealing two bags of flour, though soon released. The family's reputation had sunk to rock bottom but, even in more and more distressed circumstances, they somehow retained a spirited, non-reproachful dignity and a noticeably compassionate attitude towards one another, manifested in (and perhaps succoured by) their nightly habit of fervidly praying together. *Family Prayers in Le Cachot* (see page 75) with its strong flowing verticals, shows their unified dignity of spirit and purpose within the stark, rough-hewn interior. Unlike their serious elders, especially the nobly patient, subtly anguished François, the two young boys have a charmingly impish glint in their eyes, whilst remaining spiritually utterly in tune with the rest of the family.

Bernadette, Shepherdess at Bartrès

IN September 1857, Bernadette went to live with her old wet-nurse Marie Laguës at Bartrès, where she worked as babysitter, maid and shepherdess. Conditions were tough there; her regular morning and evening meal was one of corn paste, which she had long found indigestible. She had to work hard for meagre sustenance in difficult times. Laurentin has written: 'She…never sulked about her work. What hurt her most was…that she had come on the understanding that she would at last be able to study her catechism…with the parish priest. But the place of a shepherdess is always with her sheep.'

Greg is very aware that, as was the case with his treatment of St Francis and Kaspar Hauser, so with Bernadette he is dealing with different aspects of her character; and all the time, impressively diverse archetypal facets seem to emerge. In *The Courtyard, Working at Bartrès* (see page 95), Bernadette appears, says Greg, 'as a very strong woman grappling; I have this feeling of a peasant strength, almost touching on another aspect, that of an Athene-like goddess, who has this rich, strong, earthy presence.' The muddy courtyard, aptly conjured up through spontaneous ink strokes, is sparely irradiated by soft blue tones, as are Bernadette's figure, a glisteningly blue-eyed cockerel and the heavy spade itself, which seems to be not only digging up the soil but piercing through to the heart of the world itself! The old millstone standing behind similarly sparkles with blue, taking on an appearance perhaps as a cosmic wheel of light.

As a shepherdess in the hills above Bartrès, Bernadette spent many solitary hours with her dog, Pigou (see page 93), and the lambs. One of the latter, her favourite, would ceaselessly knock over the little altars she would build (a local custom in May). She held no grudge against him, saying, 'To punish him, I would give him a little salt, of which he was very fond.' *The Shepherdess* (see page 37) was the first picture Greg made of Bernadette. It shows her in a headscarf, her pet lamb in her arms in a quite maternal embrace. 'It's quite windy. Springtime. Quite a mysterious, questioning

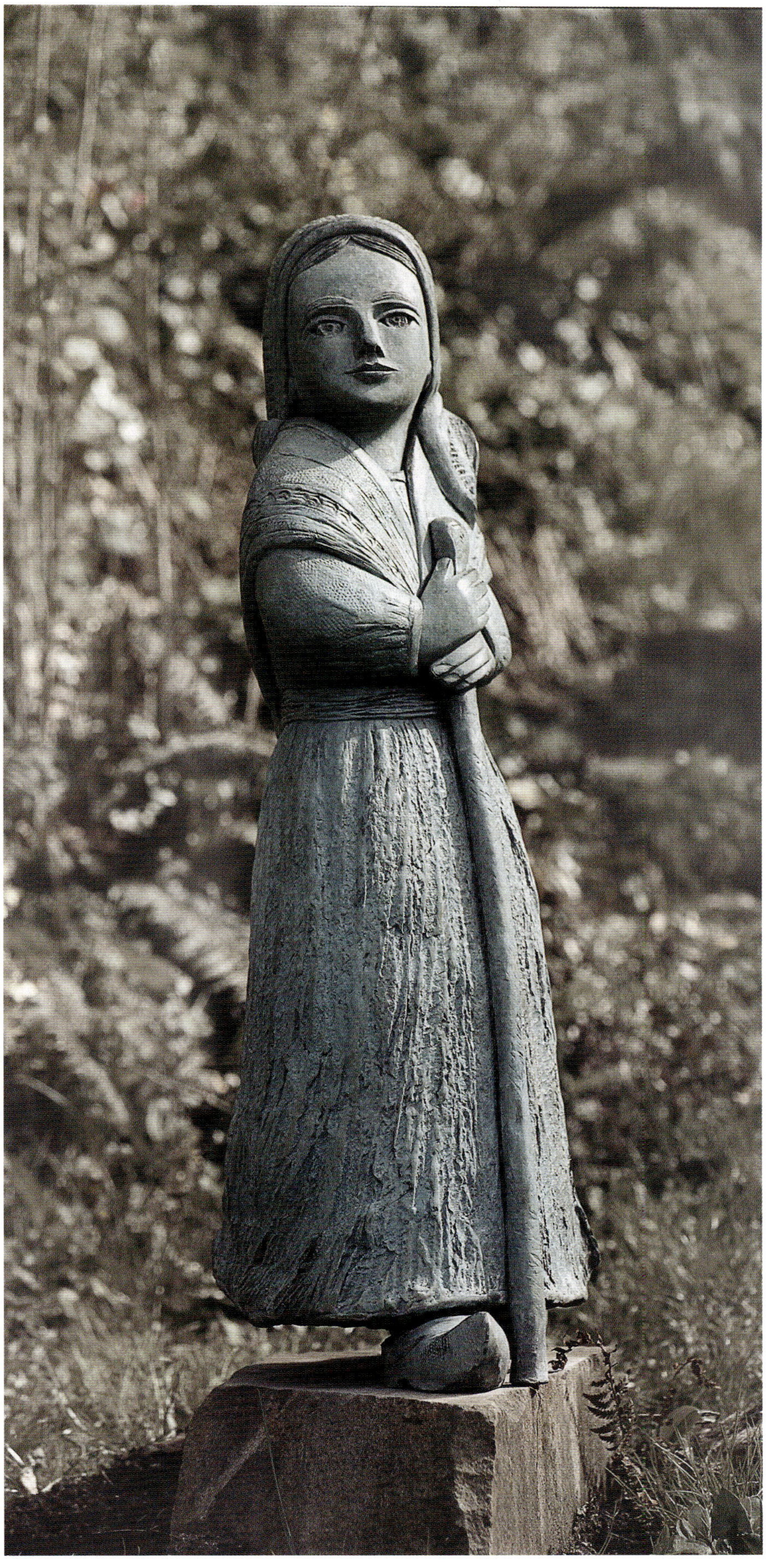

The Shepherdess, 40 x 20 x 12 inches, bronze

picture. It shows an elemental connection with the feminine, with Mother Earth, you could say, a connection which has, by its nature, an earthiness, windiness, airiness, a sense of healing waters. It's this connection which is a driving force.' These elemental qualities manifest throughout the picture, even, in this land-locked scene, a sense of 'healing waters' in the varied blue tones present in Bernadette's clothes and features. Painting this work 'was when the blue first came to me. At first I thought she was holding lavender. And actually it was the blue of lavender. And then I realised it was the lamb. This was the first picture, you could say, divining what it was to be.'

THE sculpture *Shepherdess* (see page 25), with its soft verdigris patina which melds beautifully with surrounding greenery when seen *en plein air*, is the first bronze that Greg has made. He found the paradoxically reverse process of making it as fresh and revelatory as he had initially found the batik-painting process. He made it first in clay, 'which was so different to working from the stone. The stone is solid and grounded from the beginning. But the clay is so malleable and easily impressionable. It felt very strange to see the original model crumbling, cracked and discarded after a wax cast had been made in the foundry, from which eventually the bronze was cast.' *Shepherdess* shows Bernadette on the hills about Bartrès, her small stature appearing sturdily and nobly upright, the strong vertical of her stick perhaps matched by the line of her far-seeing eye, her clear gaze able to look out for her sheep at a distance. Her subtle strength is conveyed here, her character which Greg describes as that of a 'sensitive, slightly hidden person, very honest, strong and humourous. Somehow this little girl managed to stand up against the most immense authorities of her day, and just brushed it all aside. It was incredible.'

The atmosphere in the wet-nurse's house at Bartrès grew increasingly oppressive, with the death of the wet-nurse's son (re-opening all the traumatic wounds too of the death of Marie Laguës' first-born son thirteen years before, after which she had agreed to nurse Bernadette). Then Bernadette's hope of cathechism lessons was dashed. She told her parents she was 'sick and tired' of Bartrès, a rare criticism coming from her which François and Louise knew to take seriously. In January 1858, Bernadette returned to La Cachot, to its dreadful living conditions but also to the affection of her family.

François in Bed (see page 97), showing the hungry miller lying down, his face etched with distress, is an archetypal depiction of pity and affliction. He has retired to bed to save the little food he has for his family. His starved grimace is taut and inward-looking. The bleak darkness of the room and his situation is shown by the palette inclining to black and murky brown. However, his figure and features are outlined, as if in reverse, by a glowingly sensitive meandering white line, and his face is irradiated by the chalky white of inner illumination. Indeed, the subject of such a picture can also be said to be the mysterious paradox at the heart of the *via negativa* evoked often in Christian mystical literature: in Dionysius the Areopagite's words: 'The Divine Dark is the inaccessible Light in which God is said to dwell.'

Bernadette Looks Out (see page 83) depicts Bernadette peering from behind a door at us, and the world beyond, half resolutely focussed, half indistinctly introspective. This is what the artist calls 'a threshold picture', full of questioning, as her young, round, fresh face stands on the verge of whole new dimensions of existence. Her gaze into the unknown poses as many questions for her as it does for us, the viewers. Her white scarf laps over her shoulders like a crest of a wave, or maybe the wing of a bird about to set flight. The simple, earthy yet subtly applied palette of blues, greens, white and browns is given piquancy and vibrancy by the few lines and touches of orange, notably above her left eye.

Bernadette meets Mary

ON Thursday 11th February 1858, Bernadette, breathless with asthma, insisted on leaving the confines of home to get some fresh rural air. With her sister Marie-Toinette and a friend, Jeanne, she went out searching for firewood. They eventually came to a sandy point where the River Gave rejoins the canal that turns the Savy mill. Michel de Saint-Pierre has written: 'They crossed the lovely La Fitte meadow and found themselves almost opposite the old rocky mass... known locally as the Massabielle. There were three large caverns...One of them was a proper grotto with an arched entrance about twelve...feet high. The width of this cave was about the same as its depth, between forty and fifty feet... Within a sort of oval niche [grew] a sturdy, spreading bush... A wild briar climbed up the rock... It was a wild and desolate spot.' Her companions went off searching for wood, and Bernadette took off her clogs and stockings in order to wade across the water. Within the opening of the grotto she had a vision (as de Saint-Pierre reports she then told her companions) of 'a lady dressed in white, a lady of sixteen or seventeen years old. She had a white dress on, drawn in at the waist by a blue sash. She had a white veil on her head and falling down her back. You could hardly see her hair at all. Her feet were bare and there was a yellow rose on each of them. On her right arm there was a rosary of white beads...and the chain was golden, all shining like the two roses at her feet.'

Marie-Toinette could not resist telling her mother news of the apparition. Louise at first chided her but Bernadette was so persistent about what she had seen that she soon stopped trying to convince her daughter she was mistaken. But she demanded that Bernadette should not return to Massabielle. However, on the following Sunday, she went along with six of her companions to the very same spot; news spread fast and soon there was a whole procession accompanying her. She knelt again at the right of the grotto facing the bush above which the Lady had appeared. She now re-appeared. Tremulously, Bernadette said: 'If you come from God, come nearer!' She attempted but found her self unable to say: 'If you come from the Devil, go away.' The Lady smiled graciously at her with an almost unimaginable affection. These two visions were the first of many apparitions which occurred on her visits to the grotto—increasingly attended by growing crowds of local people, and then from all over the country—until Bernadette's eighteenth vision took place on 16th July in the Ribière meadow (near the grotto, which by now had been barricaded off by the anxious civil authorities, perturbed by the vast if respectful crowds that gathered each time Bernadette visited the spot).

Many eye-witnesses, including sceptics, attested to the blissful happiness, the infinitely tender smile evident on Bernadette's face as she alone saw the vision of the Lady in the grotto, her ecstasies lasting sometimes for an hour. One witness (quoted by de Saint-Pierre) noted: 'The raised eyes are wide open, looking...ecstatically upwards. Not a tremor moves her eyelids... Occasionally the lips move visibly, but only slightly... Now and again two tears roll down her cheeks like drops of dew.' On one occasion, in tears she repeated several times to the crowds words which the Lady had spoken to her: 'Penitence! Penitence! Penitence!' Then a local sergeant demanded of her: 'What do you think you're up to, my little joker!' Bernadette made no reply but just went on praying. The sergeant then angrily turned to his men to say: 'To think that this is the 19th century and to see such stupidity!'

Bernadette said that the Lady told her secrets but, as secrets, these could not be passed on to anyone, not even the Pope. As de Saint-Pierre recalls, '"When the Blessed Virgin told me the secrets she did not speak to my ears but here," and Bernadette pointed to her heart.'

On the 25th March, Bernadette felt impelled to visit the grotto. The ecclesiastical authorities had demanded that, on her next visionary encounter, she enquire who the Lady is. Four times on this meeting, Bernadette asked the smiling Lady, 'Mademoiselle, would you be so kind as to tell me who you are, if you please?' The Lady stopped smiling and laughing and announced in the *patois* of Lourdes in which they spoke:

'Que soy era Immaculata Concepciou.' 'I am the Immaculate Conception.'

IN *Meeting the Lady* (see page 99), Bernadette appears as a grounded, relaxed figure in dark brown and blue attire, one arm softly resting on another, as she gazes up at the tall figure in profile, a woman in ethereal white, her lips slightly parted as if in the most tenderly benevolent communication. This picture exudes an ineffable sweetness and delicacy of both feeling and application. To the top left, eglantine is seen growing. Greg says that 'the picture didn't feel right until the eglantine appeared, endowing the picture with an atmosphere of intimacy which helped resolve the picture, suddenly placing the viewer in amongst Bernadette and Mary. It's almost as if we've moved to Mary's side somehow, and there's a profound shift of perception from Bernadette's perspective to the point where we actually feel we are seeing the world through Mary's eyes. Water is seen coming through the mountain.'

The limestone sculpture of *Bernadette in Prayer* (see page 29), showing her with hands raised and clasped in prayer, has an airy whiteness, resolute refinement and seeming transparency about it, qualities curiously quite close in feeling to those in the representation of Mary in *Meeting the Lady*. The sculpture has simultaneously an archaic, even medieval look to it and a modernist succinctness of style.

The Healing Spring (see page 101) perhaps stands at the metaphysical centre of the paintings in this series. As in *Meeting the Lady*, Mary stands in gently imposing profile to the right. Bernadette stands to the left with her iridescently outlined right hand reaching a point on the rock, from whence a spring flows. At this meeting on 25th February, the Lady had directed Bernadette, in Greg's words, 'to go and dig where the moss and rocks were. So gradually water came out, and the spring has been going ever since. The water now pours out. It is rather remarkable that the spring didn't appear before Bernadette uncovered it.' The graceful gestural poise of Bernadette's delicately elongated hand as it touches the grotto side, is counterbalanced by the gushing, plashy spontaneity from an unseen source, seen as a rush of light from within the rockface; (the effect is rather like that made by Greg's portrayal of the sun-illumined dove of peace glimpsed by St Francis through the small window in his dark, mossy cell at Carceri Hermitage). Mary and Bernadette's singular eyes in profile are transfixed by the moment of fresh creativeness, as finger touches rock. The range of deep olive and emerald greens ('colours very special to me') help evoke the elemental nature of this amazing occurrence taking place in wooded, grassy, mossy nature. The strong mix of lights and darks here contributes to the picture's transfiguring effect, like that of medieval stained glass. Certainly as depicted in this picture, these waters appear as a healing wellspring, a radiant light, the mystical essence of life itself. Bernadette's response to this vision was humbling. At the various ecclesiastical and civil interviews she had to undergo to establish the truth of her vision, and where she conveyed the insistence communicated to her, she said, by Mary, that a church be built in the grotto, she made no claims about the value of her experiences nor about the curative properties of the uncovered spring. She simply related what she had seen and felt with astonishing directness, without guile, and sometimes with a humour

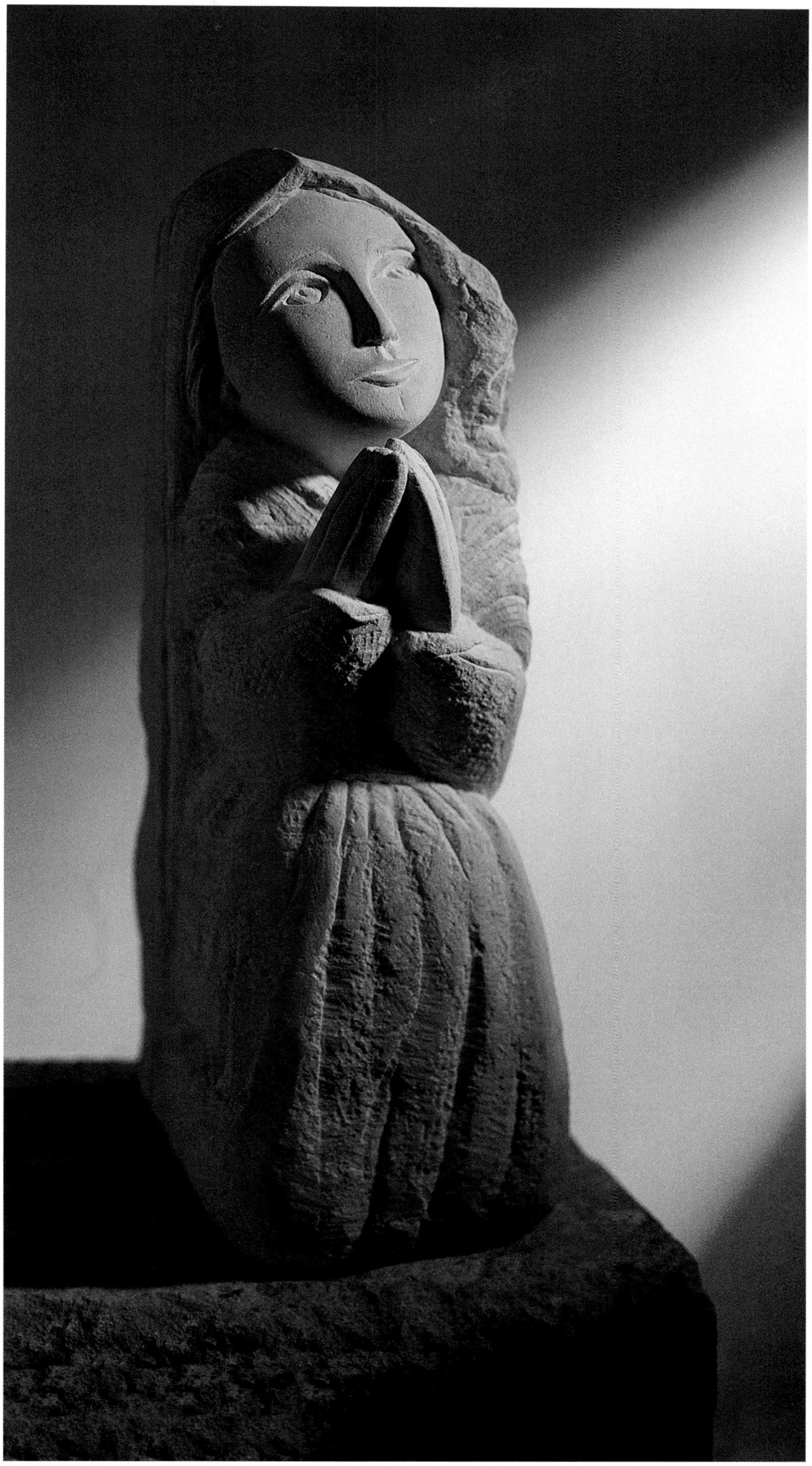

Bernadette in Prayer, 23 x 7 x 12 inches, Portland Stone

that perplexed and deflated the interrogating authorities. She was once asked, relates de Saint-Pierre, '"The water of the Grotto cures other people; why doesn't it cure you?

> "Perhaps the Blessed Virgin wants me to go on suffering."
> "Why do you think she could want that?"
> "Perhaps I need to suffer."
> "Why should you need to suffer more than others?"
> "The good God would know that."'

By this stage, she simply wanted to be left alone at the grotto, a lively-minded, not at all sanctimonious fifteen-year old girl with her prayers and memories, but the Lourdes phenomenon had taken on a wider life of its own, and was undoubtedly reaching out inexorably to a need for healing in increasing numbers of people. Greg says he sees something in the Bernadette series of 'the Sophia spirit of wisdom [Sophia the goddess of wisdom in ancient Greek philosophy as well as goddess of the divine feminine in the Judaeo-Christian tradition], almost beyond time, that mystically resonates in Mary. This comes back maybe to the origins of my work. I do feel that it relates to something in our age that is calling for rebirth. I think my work makes a stand for the spirit. As time has gone on in our society, the patriarchal elements have taken over, and I feel my work pushes that back a little, opening up the veil towards what I call the eternal feminine.' This latter quality is not necessarily related to gender, since, in their fertile openness of spirit and attitudes of caring intimacy, both St Francis[16] and Kaspar Hauser (the least fossilised or patriarchal of figures) undoubtedly partook of this spirit. These lines from Gerard Manley Hopkins' poem, *The Blessed Virgin compared to the Air we Breathe*, equate to the elemental and redemptive atmosphere of Greg's Bernadette series:

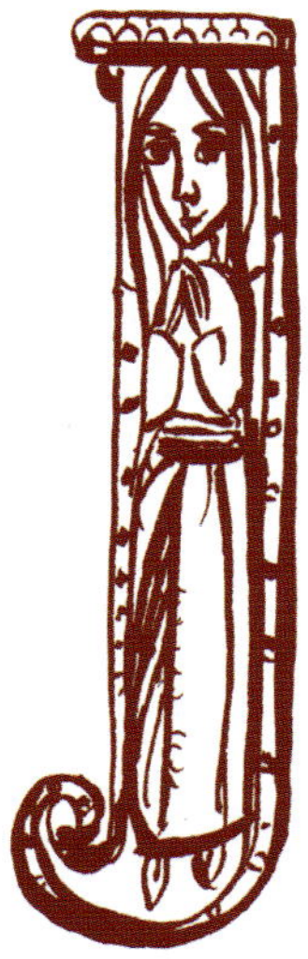

Mary Immaculate,
Merely a woman, yet
Whose presence, power is
Great as no goddess's
Was deeméd, dreamed; who
This one work has to do –
Let all God's glory through

Worldmothering air, air wild,
Wound with thee, in thee isled,
Fold home, fast fold thy child.

Girl with the Apple - Le Cachot (see page 115) shows Bernadette's own 'worldmothering air' (to use Hopkins' fine, idiosyncratic phrase) as she attends to a six-year-old girl whose arms were partially paralysed. Bernadette kept placing the apple in the girl's jolting palm. The shy little girl left, not cured but smiling, feeling reassured by the devoted attention given by Bernadette. The emphatically exaggerated but not unnatural eyes of Bernadette and the child are the picture's serene focal points, contrasting with the averted, downcast or anxious miens of the other two women portrayed.

A SENSE of 'Mary immaculate' caring for Bernadette in her domestic life is conveyed in *Ave Maria* (see page 79). Bernadette sits on a simple rustic chair, holding a Cross in one hand and rosary beads in the other. Her Lady, barefoot, kneels at the side, her head gracefully inclining towards the young girl. This iconic picture is actually one of the most adventurous in Greg's series, since it imagines a meeting of the two at Le Cachot, where none of the apparitions are known to have taken place. But there is a poetic and spiritual truth here in that Bernadette was undoubtedly nurtured by her experience of Mary while dwelling in this dismal though not unloving home. Her closeness with Mary was ubiquitous. Seeing the prison bars in this picture adds a desperately haunting note here, relating Bernadette to other key figures throughout Greg's oeuvre, and to these lines (already quoted from W.H. Auden):

> *In the prison of his days*
> *Teach the free man how to praise.*

Bernadette eschewed any public responses to news of her visions, though these mounted all the time. Gifts and any notoriety were anathema to her. When someone tried to give her a golden coin, she responded, 'It burns me.' One day, a queue of fashionable folk had gathered at the door of Le Cachot. *Waiting to See Bernadette* (see page 109) is a curiously satiric work, with a mild but striking touch of Ensor-esque or Rouault-like caricature, pitting the quite comically inquisitive-looking wealthy women in their hooped skirts, jewellery and fine hats against the figure of Bernadette, with her decorously inclined head, her rosary beads, her long blue scarf flowing like a stream, and her long black dress (its black colour subtly glinting with streaks of purple, green and pink, hinting at an interior richness). In *Skipping at Lourdes Hospice* (see page 119), we see another, wilder aspect of Bernadette, in the leaping high spirits of an adolescent girl as she soars above the cobblestones in the presence of nuns and hospice patients. Whether in her restrained or wild-looking guise, Bernadette seems to retain imperturbable inner assurance.

Bernadette enters Nevers Convent

IN July 1858, Bernadette left Lourdes by train for the last time to become a novice at the Saint-Gildard Convent in Nevers, sightseeing at Bordeaux and Périgueux on the way. The mistress of novices allowed Bernadette to recount the story of her encounters at the grotto to three hundred nuns from this and nearby convents, insisting that thereafter these should not be mentioned. *Bernadette Enters Nevers Convent* (see page 123) shows the young peasant girl in her ordinary costume and clogs with Mother Marie-Thérèse Vauzou holding a bible, and two other senior nuns flanking her. What is noticeable, in severe contrast to the dark confines of Le Cachot, is the pristine clerical order and lightness of the space, with its red-and-white checkerboard floor, the nuns' austere habits (though the black is irradiated slightly by a redemptive blue), the white, barely criss-cross patterned walls, and the big open windows. There is a quizzical though amiable sharpness in the aspects of the nuns greeting Bernadette; she was to find herself often gently chided, sometimes miserably misunderstood for her independence of spirit, clearly evident in this portrayal.

She suffered persistent ill-health, and entered the convent infirmary quite often suffering from asthma and fatigue. When she was well enough, she herself worked in the infirmary, tending the sick with great dedication. For her, at least until her health latterly worsened, the great trials were unwelcome visits from curious visitors; she would think up various ruses to evade them, either in person or at least conversationally.

IN January 1873 Bernadette was suffering badly from asthma. It wasn't until 12th May that she felt well enough to embark on a trip by horse and carriage with Mother Joséphine Imbert. In *Visit to Varennes Orphanage*, which depicts her receiving flowers from a little girl (see page 129), the human group (the two nuns, three children) take up a small part of the composition towards the far right. This grouping is still the dramatic focus in a picture full of other affectionately rendered arrangements within a wide, spacious pastoral view: two trees to the far left, then two trees diminutive in the distance; intercepting the pairs of trees, a church and cottages; the horse and cart at the centre of the composition; a spade lying on the earth next to a trough in which grow wild flowers. The way the picture is composed seems to indicate that each grouping is equally special; each is vitally important in the wider scheme of things. Bernadette said to the orphans: 'My children, have real love for the holy Virgin… Pray to her conscientiously. She will protect you.'

The principle of 'the eternal feminine'—revealed in many religions, and transcending any cultural divides—is beautifully summed up in the words of the Buddha: 'Like a mother who protects her child, her only child, with her own life, one should cultivate a heart of unlimited love and compassion to all living beings.'

Bernadette's gaiety was not at all extinguished in the convent; on occasion, it thrived, though she was disappointed to learn that she was not allowed to do skipping there. *Rolling Carrots* (see page 127) shows her and fellow nuns at the moment when Bernadette by mistake had sent a plate of sliced carrots flying all over the refectory table and the floor. It is a moment of exuberant disarray and consequent unrestrained hilarity on the nuns' part. As in other paintings of Bernadette, the use of orange adds a vibrant note to scenes otherwise restrained in colour. There is a flavour of the Holy Fool in this portrayal of Bernadette in her generous playfulness, and the rejection of a staid response to the spilling out of nature's abundance. Greg says, 'I think Bernadette was a sort of Holy Fool in a way because when she was confronted all the time by the authorities, she had such honest answers. She would answer so honestly, it was hilarious. They would accuse her: "how do you know it was Mary talking to you and not just the bird chirping?" And she would say, "if it was a bird, it wouldn't have spoken to me, would it." So there was this radical Holy Fool aspect to Bernadette.'

Bernadette with Flowers (see page 131) shows her placing a vase of flowers on the altar before a statue of Mary. The clarity of her figure in black and white against the faded white chapel backdrop brings her aesthetic devotional act—she had loved decorating altars since early childhood—into vivid relief. Greg says he especially appreciated painting the medieval figurative carvings at the base of the altar, so worn and intangibly evocative compared to the starkly realised person of Bernadette herself.

In 1876, asked whether she wished to revisit her native town, she said, 'I have sacrificed Lourdes. I will see the holy Virgin in heaven. That will be more beautiful.' When she was shown photographs of the newly reconstructed grotto, she reacted sadly: 'Oh, my poor grotto! I would not recognise it any more.' From this time on, she suffered extended periods of ill health, often confined to bed. In her letters to friends, she always stressed how well she was cared for at Nevers, indeed like 'a little baby'. When she was feeling well enough in fine weather, she would spend long hours doing embroidery work in a sheltered corner of the cloister. In *Bernadette's*

Embroidery (see page 133), light seems to spill over the grey stones walls, over Bernadette's grey habit and onto the cloth itself in the form of manifold crosses, sparkling perhaps with the delight of her lucid absorption in the task at hand. There is an echo here of the poet George Herbert's phrase about how 'A servant with this clause [namely a mindful or prayerful attitude]/ Makes Drudgerie divine.'

Bernadette said: 'Jesus demands the abandonment of all possessions, of all honour, of all creatures, but the kindness of Jesus makes the parting less difficult.' *The White Chapel* (see page 135), a picture of infinite gentleness, shows the dying Bernadette. There is a poignant affinity here with Gwen John's acutely sensitive portrayals in crayon or watercolour or chalk of a *Dying Nun* clasping a crucifix (dating from the mid-late 1910s, when, living in France, Gwen turned increasingly to the Catholic Church and is known to have visited Lourdes twice). Indeed, Gwen's oil portraits of nuns, notably the enigmatically serene, rather magisterial Mère Poussepin, another of a fresh, open-faced novice *Little Nun*, and her intimately informal gouache and watercolour back views of French nuns and orphan schoolgirls, all have a mysterious, affectionate sincerity about them close in spirit to Greg's explorations of Bernadette's life.

Suffering from painful bone disease and severe asthma, the dying Bernadette was bedridden, and had the few pictures and objects in the White Chapel removed, retaining only the crucifix, saying 'That is all I need.' She felt she had been ground down like wheat. The White Chapel, where she lay, has, in Greg's hands, become transfigured into a black chamber, its drapes and Bernadette's features suffused with a range of mystical blues, like blues at Chartres delineated by powerful black binding lines. The brass finial on her bed frame has taken on the poetic presence of a golden orb. The curtains above or behind her bed have become almost like theatrical curtains opening onto another dimension, a yellowish-greenish sky with what is ambiguously a crescent moon, a full moon or even the sun itself. She is on the threshold of an unknown reality. She once said, 'Let the crucifix be not only in my eyes and on my breast but in my heart.' Her features retain their youthful prettiness and composure as she focuses on the crucifix. Bernadette died on 16th April 1879. Her last words were: 'Holy Mary, Mother of God, pray for me, poor sinner, poor sinner...'

The ultimate painting in Greg's series of works about Bernadette is *Icon - St Bernadette - The Door* (see page 137). It is actually painted over the old worn planks and hinges of a door that Greg had found. It reminded him of the door to a farm building, maybe a shepherd's hut, and, as such, was serendipitously appropriate to portray Bernadette, with hieratic frontality, as the shepherdess in the hills above Bartrès but also as a transcendent figure standing with mysterious, golden-faced serenity, with a handful of white mountain meadow flowers in her sensitively upraised hand, on the doorway, threshold to a new dimension. It may look back to those days at Bartrès but it is, ultimately, an iconic representation of Bernadette transcending, in a manner of speaking, both the story of her life and death. It portrays the essence of her perhaps, the resplendent, ever-replenishing, ever-nourishing qualities of the 'eternal feminine' which had lived in and through the figure of this young French peasant girl.

The Plates

THE SHEPHERDESS

Alone on the hillside, many hours are spent in solitude.
"It is then God speaks to the heart."

Bernadette

44 x 48½ inches
Tempera on hessian

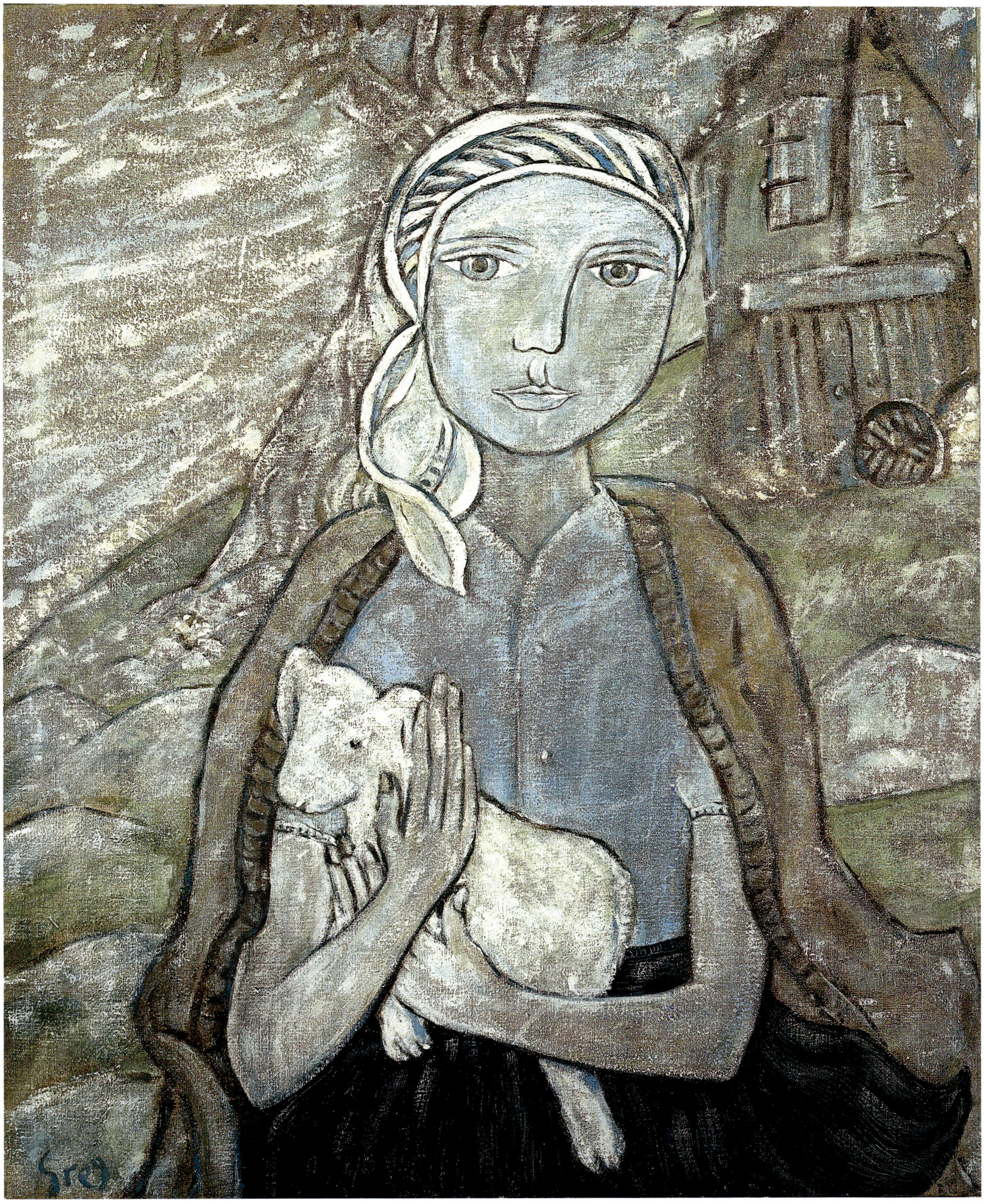

MOTHER & FATHER

BERNADETTE SOUBIROUS *was born at Boly Mill on Sunday 7th January 1844 during the hard Pyrenean winter. Bernadette's mother, Louise Castérot, was only seventeen when she married François Soubirous, a typical Bigourdan: sturdy and rugged with an expressionless face. He was twice her age when he married into the Castérot family to help run Boly Mill after Louise's father died suddenly.*

Boly Mill was one of six mills to the north of Lourdes along the tributary of the River Gave known as the Lapaca. Inside the mill, in the room adjoining the milling stones, was the traditional Basque kitchen with a large wide fireplace, a bed and a low-beamed ceiling.

15¾ x 14¼ inches
Ink and watercolour on paper

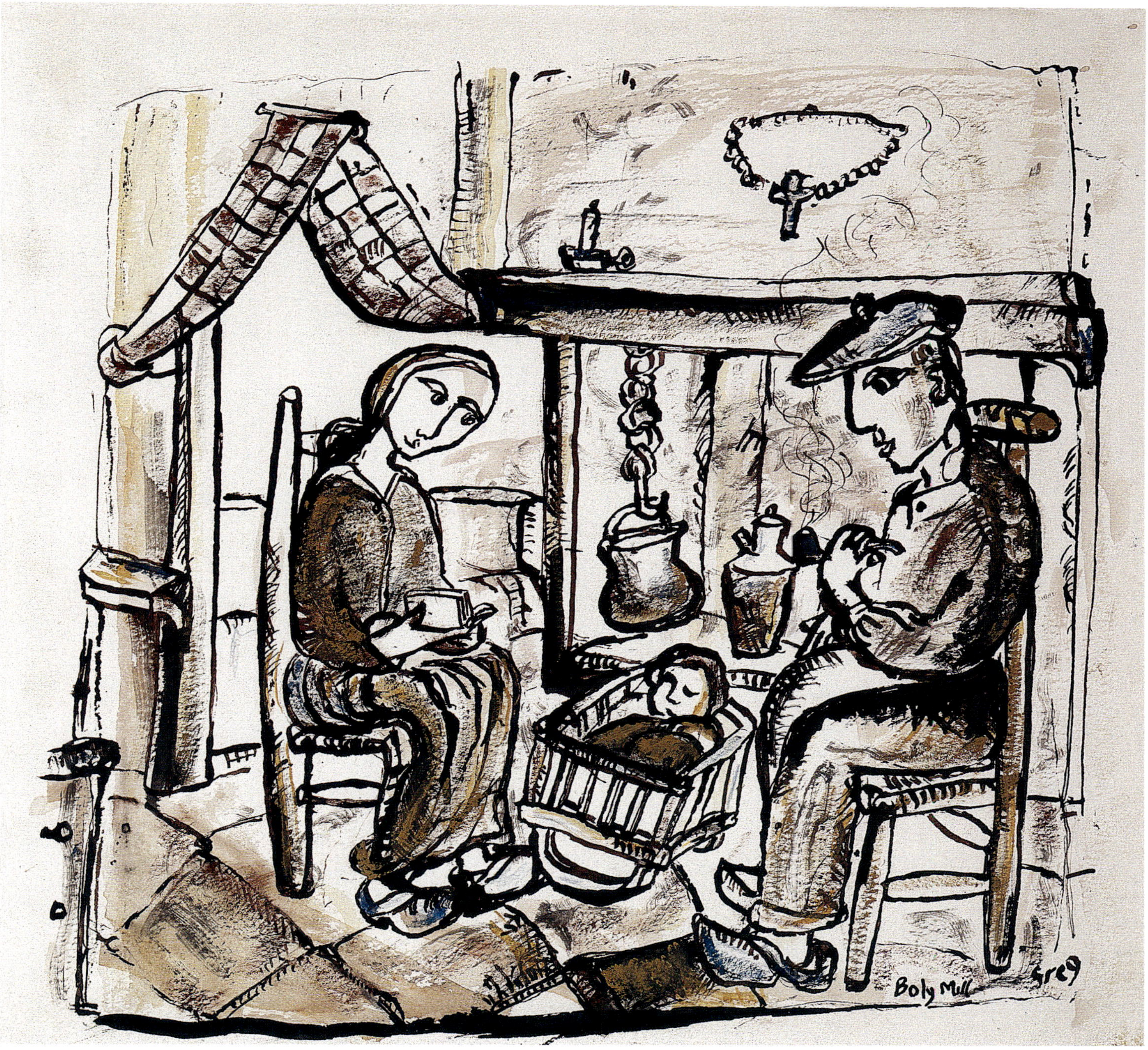
Boly Mill
Greg

THE CHRISTENING

IN LOURDES, *below the snow-capped Pyrenean mountains, joyful sounds of church bells ringing are heard as a procession of happy local Bigourdans make their way down the hill to Boly Mill, celebrating the baptism of baby Bernadette.*

She was baptized at St Peter's Church in the town square with the name Marie-Bernarde Soubirous, but she was always known as Bernadette until she entered Nevers Convent.

57½ x 34¾ inches
Oil on wood

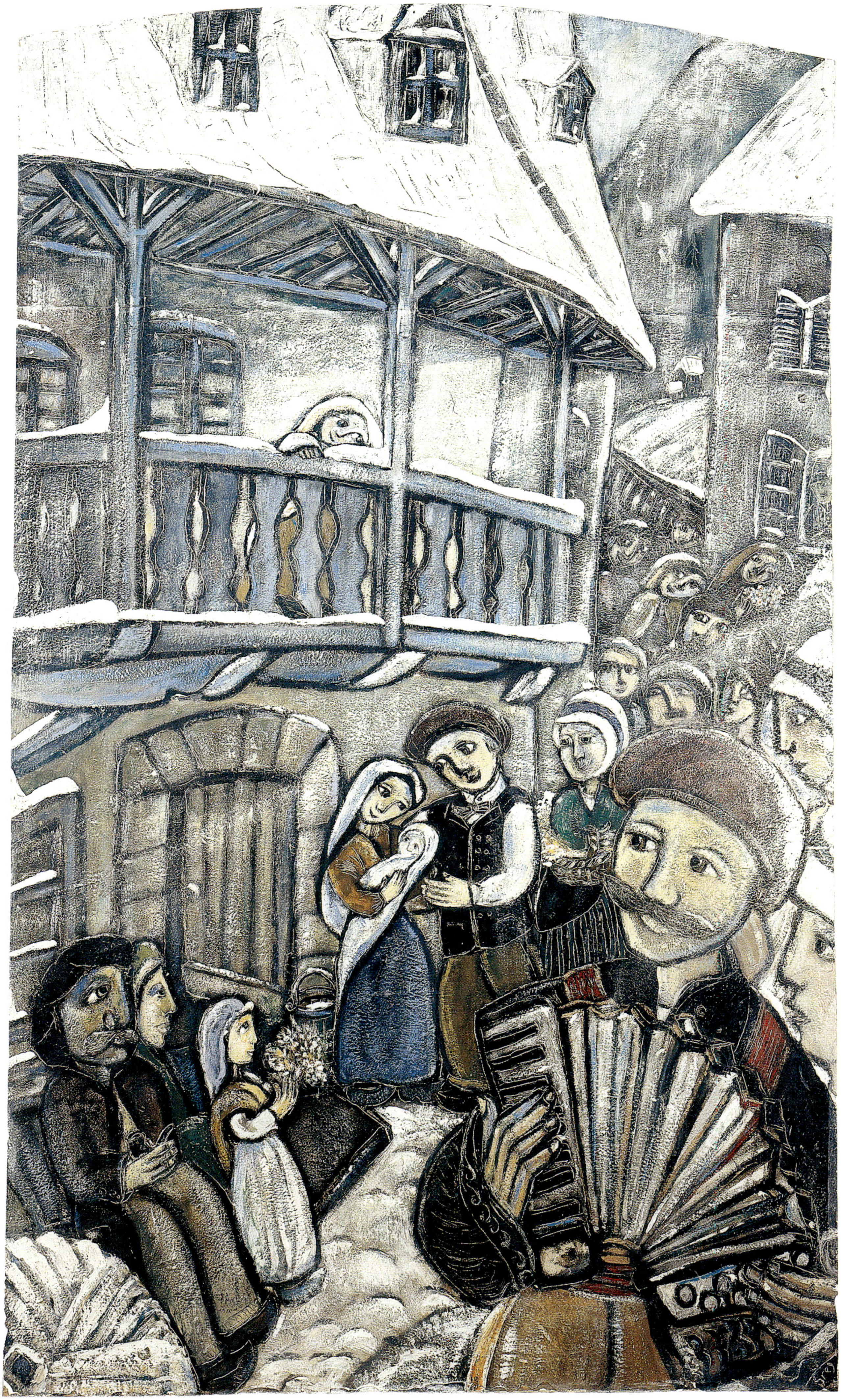

THE CHRISTENING - DETAIL

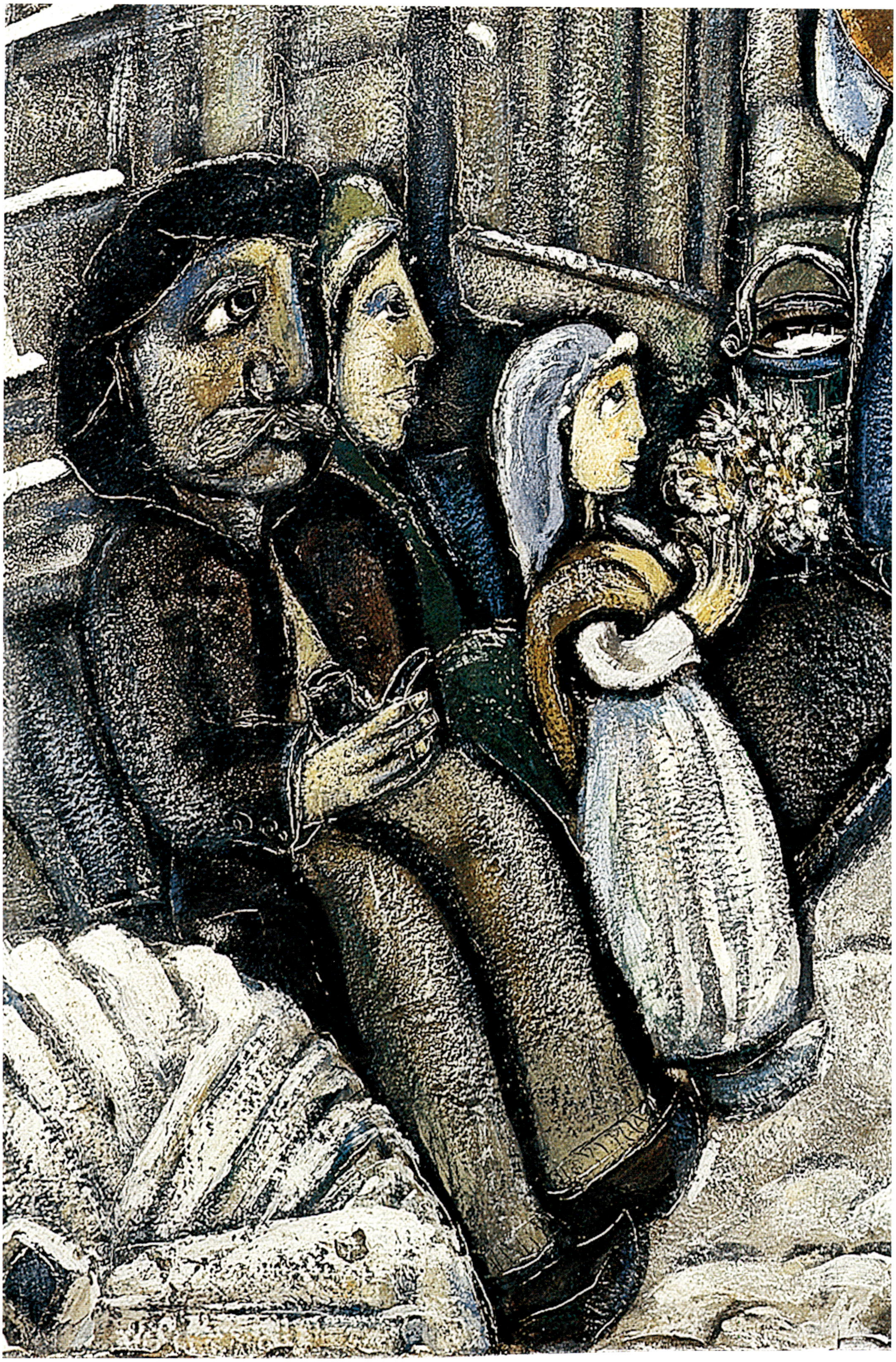

MOTHER & CHILD - BOLY MILL

33½ x 30½ inches
Oil on wood

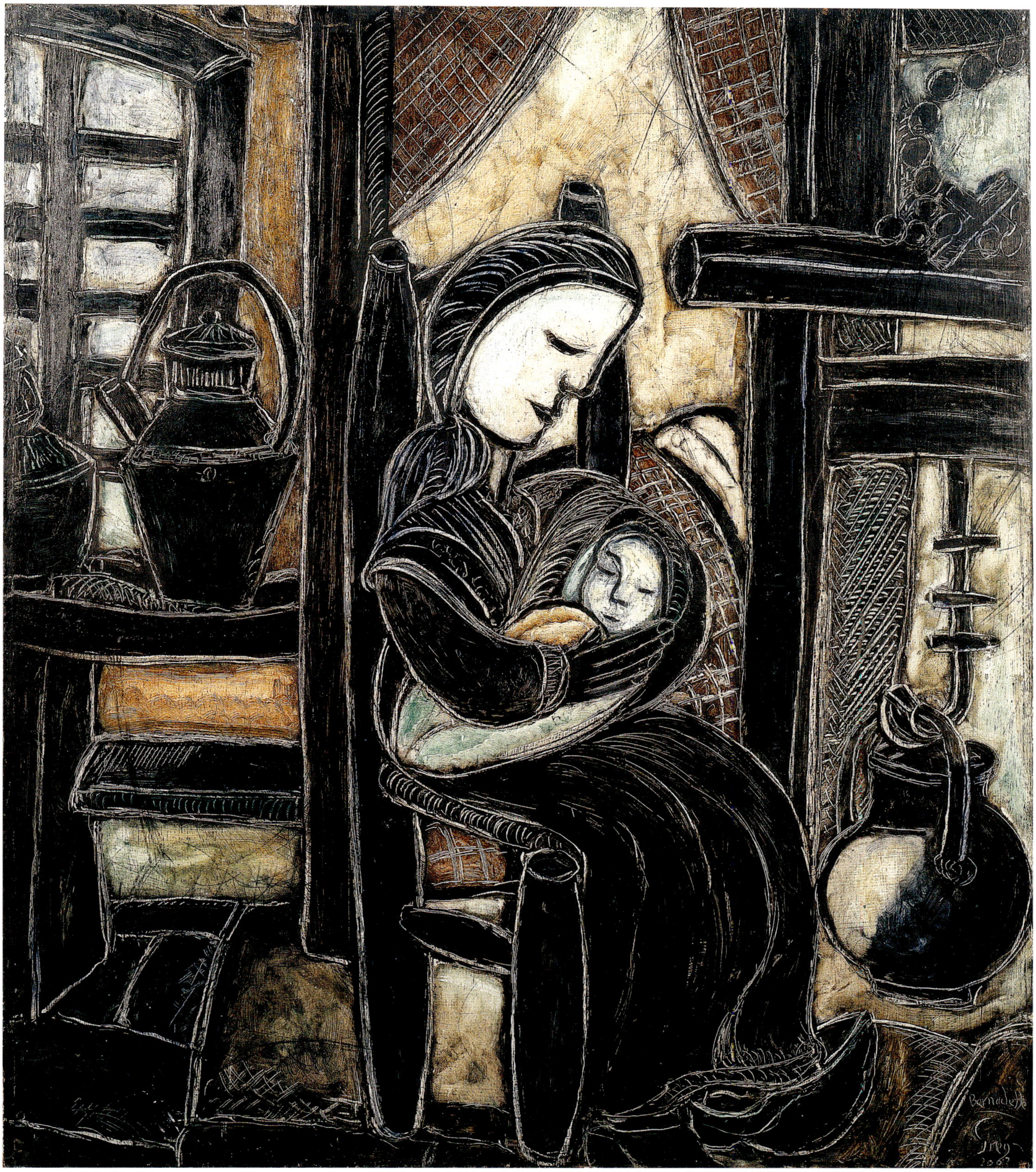
Bernadette

JOURNEY TO BARTRÈS

BERNADETTE *was only ten months old when an accident occurred whilst Louise was standing by the fireside; a stump of resin candle fell on Louise's bodice and set it alight. The burns were not severe but feeding Bernadette was difficult. She was also expecting another child, so she decided to take Bernadette, with the help of Aunt Bernarde, to be nursed by her friend Marie Laguës in the village of Bartrès three miles away. Marie looked after baby Bernadette for ten months. This gave her some comfort as her only child had died soon after birth. She was to receive payment of five francs a month in money or in flour.*

20 x 16 inches
Gouache and ink on paper

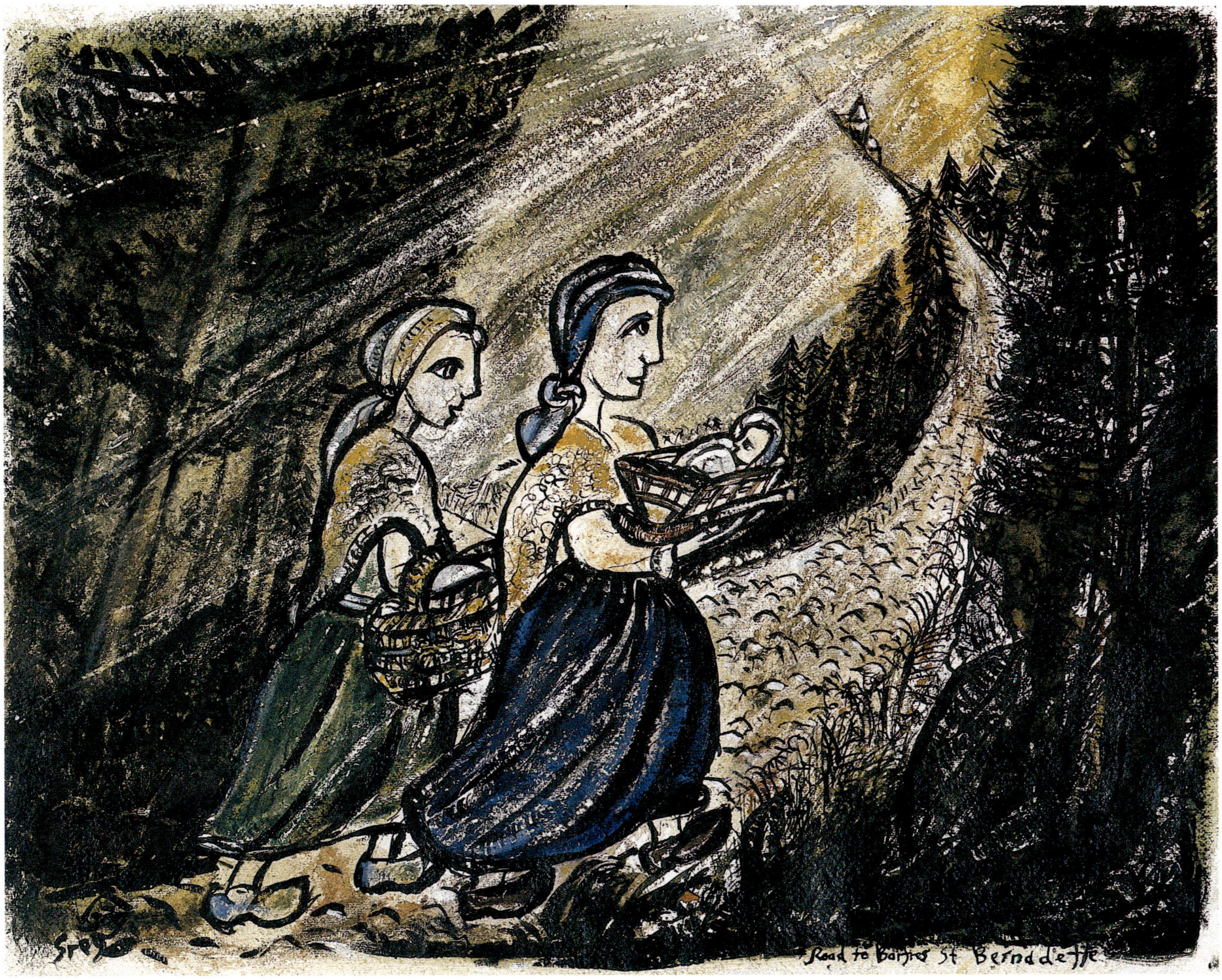
Road to Bartres St Bernadette

THE MILLER - BOLY MILL

BERNADETTE *was nearly two years old when she returned from Bartrès. She could say a number of words in the tuneful dialect of Bigorre. Her merry sounds of words mingled with the splash and rumble of the revolving millwheel, and this cheered her papa, François, all white with flour in the midst of his work.*

50¾ x 39 inches
Oil on wood

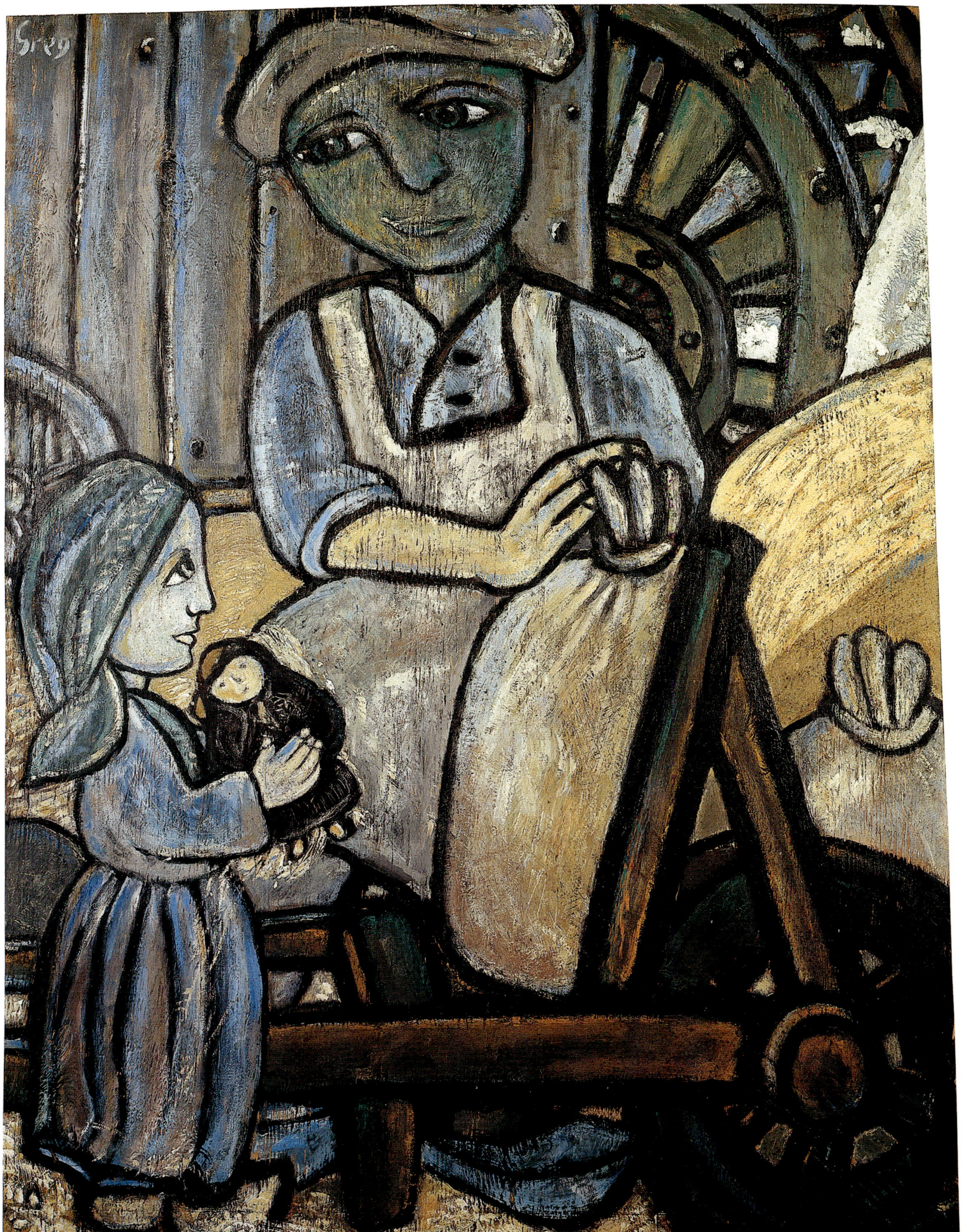

THE MARKET DAY - LOURDES

IN *the misty morning, the clatter of clogs on stones is heard as the local stoneworkers go to the slate and marble quarries. The poor women can just be seen returning from the forest of Subercarrere with bundles of wood on their heads.*

Along the banks of the River Gave, a shepherd drives his flock to pasture amongst the rocks and wastelands. The traditional fair was soon to arrive, as farm workers from the Pyrenean mountains and horse dealers from Gascony arrived at the Mercadal square. On market day Marie Laguës comes into the town from Bartrès with a surprise gift for Bernadette. Hidden in her basket at the bottom can be found some cakes!

20 x 20 inches
Gouache and ink on card

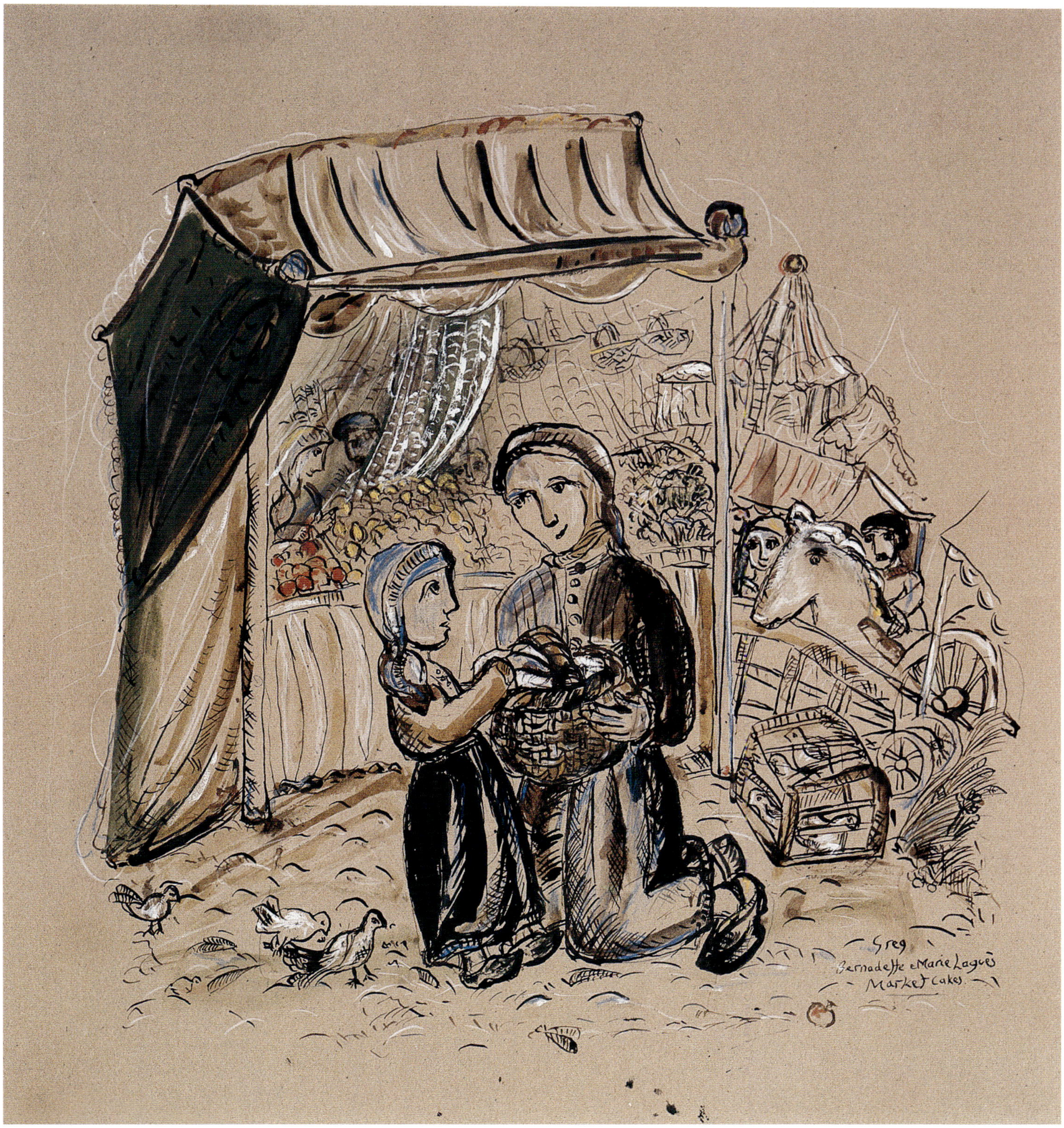
Greg
Bernadette e Marie Laguës
Market Cakes.

THE GRINDING STONES

FRANÇOIS *raised the flood gates with a powerful jerk of his stick, setting the millwheel in motion as the water flowed under Boly Mill. The large grinding stones spun round crushing the corn, fed by the hopper, into flour.*

Women from Lourdes and the neighbouring villages came with just enough corn for grinding their weekly bread.

As was the custom, a snack of bread, cheese and wine was provided by the miller while they waited. The result of this generous gesture left the Soubirous with less than they were paid. They were soon verging on bankruptcy.

29½ x 32 inches
Acrylic and pastel on hessian

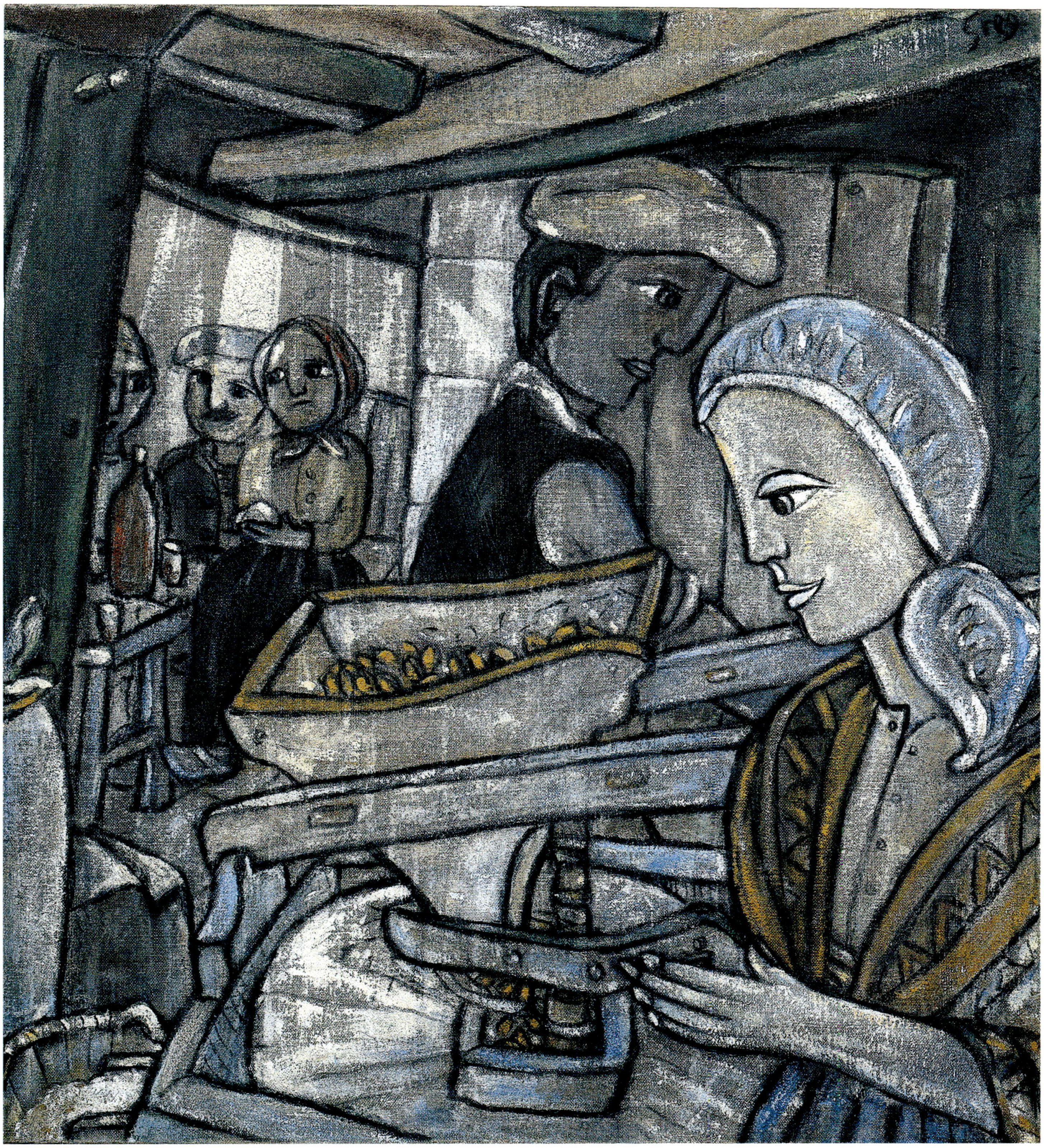

BERNADETTE & BABY JUSTIN

SMOKE *rises from the embers of the fire as Bernadette cradles her brother Justin, like a young mother. There is housework to be done as her mother and father have gone to work, leaving her with her younger sister Toinette and brother Jean-Marie.*

The family were soon to move from Lourdes to the nearby village of Arcizac-ez Angles where they rented a hut and François went to work in the local mill.

Bernadette had suffered badly at the time of the cholera epidemic sweeping through Lourdes in 1855, and was left weakened by asthma attacks that were to affect her all her life.

55¼ x 35⅛ inches
Tempera and charcoal on hessian

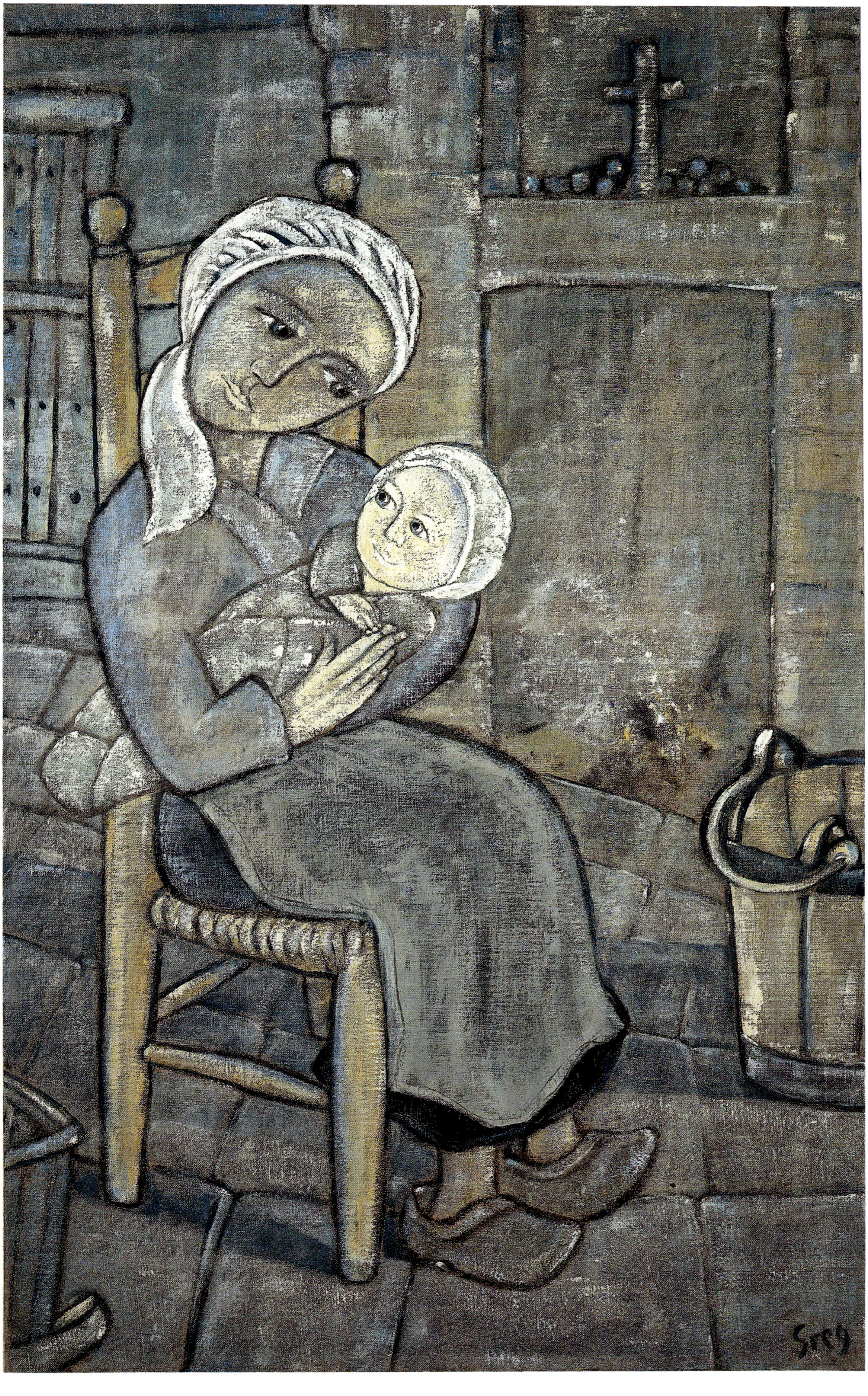

THE HARVEST HORSE & CART

*M*OTHER LOUISE *joined the peasant harvest workers in the cornfields on Mengalettes farm, not far from town. At break time she looked up, surprised to see Bernadette boldly walking through the fields carrying baby Justin. Bernadette was looking for her mother to feed the baby.*

42½ x 33 inches
Acrylic, charcoal and pastel on hessian

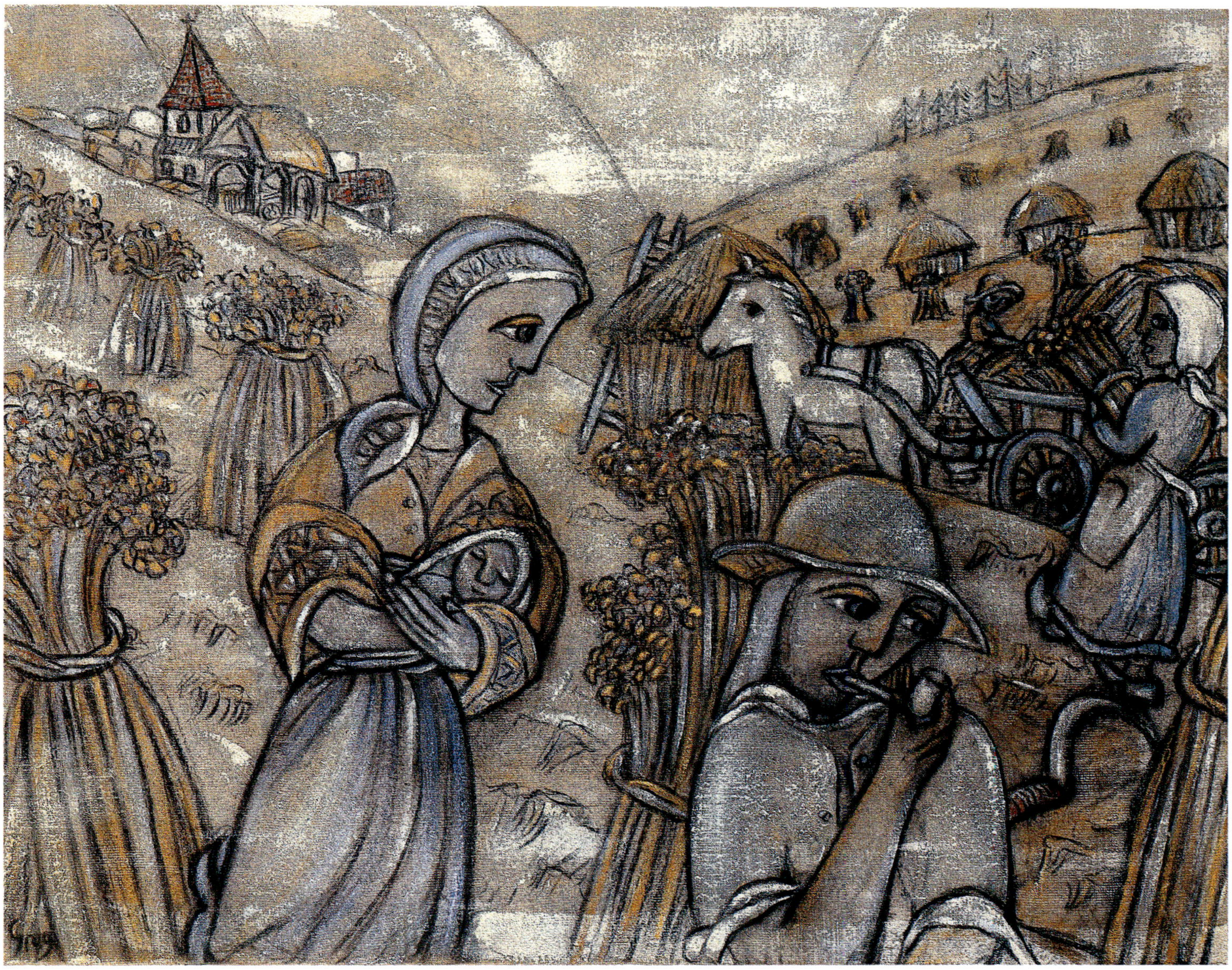

MOTHER HARVEST

A moment of peace.

40 x 48½ inches
Tempera and charcoal on canvas

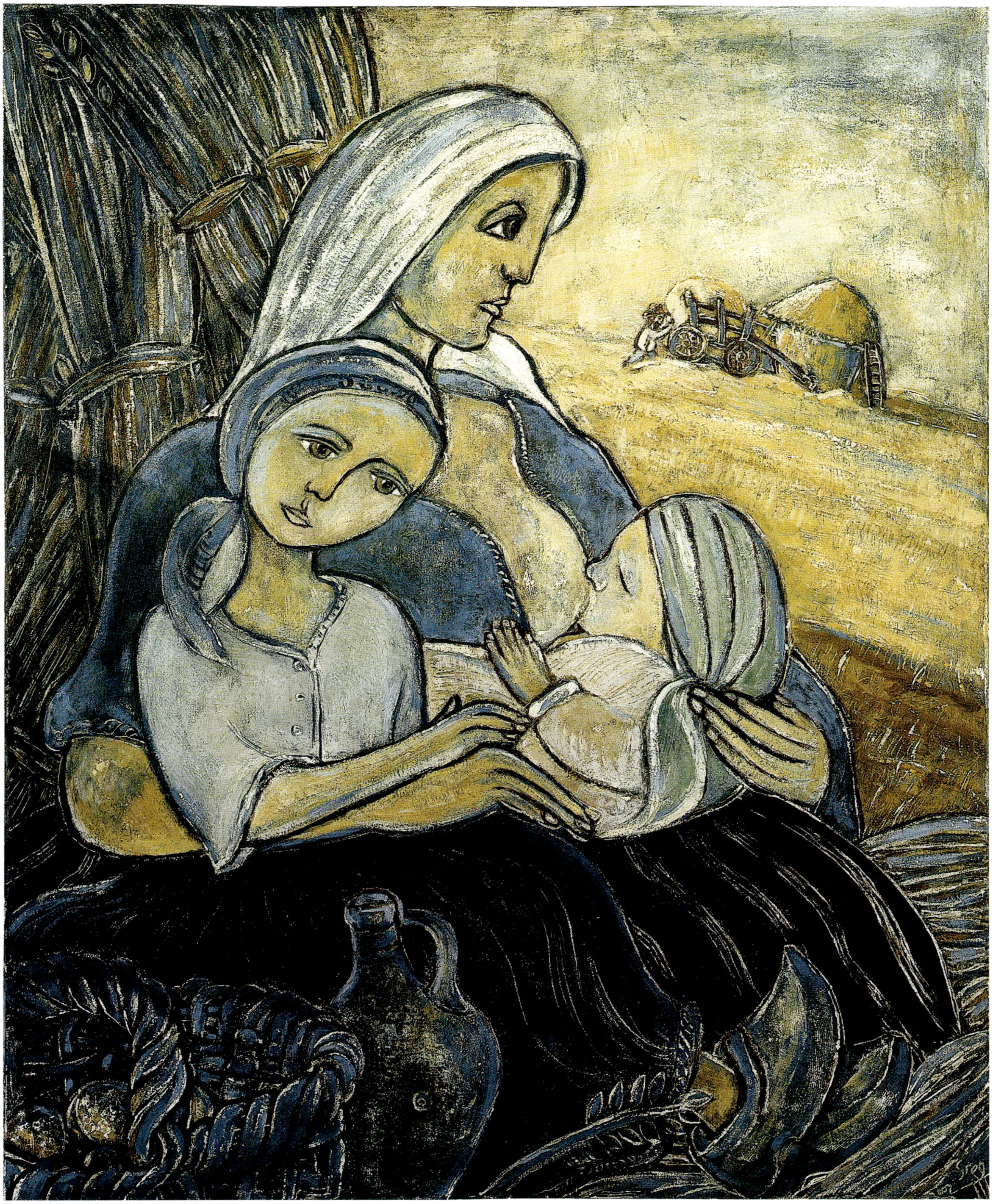

THE FLOUR CART

THE *sound of horses, hooves and cartwheels bumping on cobbled stones breaks the early morning silence in Lourdes, as François drives the flour cart trundling down the Rue du Bourg. François takes the road towards Saint-Jean-de-Luz, working for the local baker transporting flour and bread.*

He worked now as a day labourer since the family returned to Lourdes in 1856, and rented a room by the Rock of the Castle.

49¾ x 28 inches
Oil, charcoal and pastel on canvas

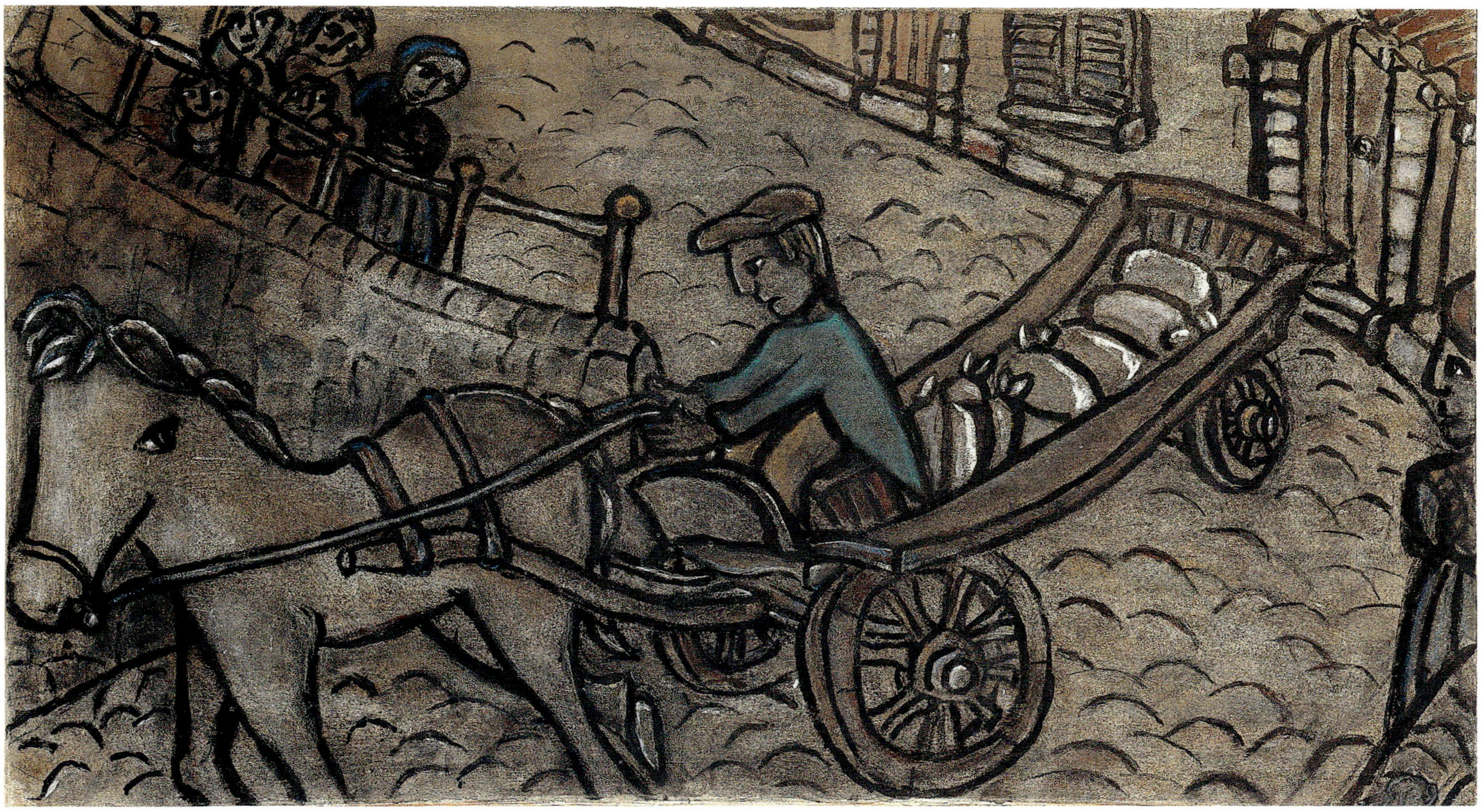

THE GOLDEN HARVEST

Like the ancient Corn Goddess, Bernadette moves through the golden harvest.

44½ x 30 inches
Oil on wood

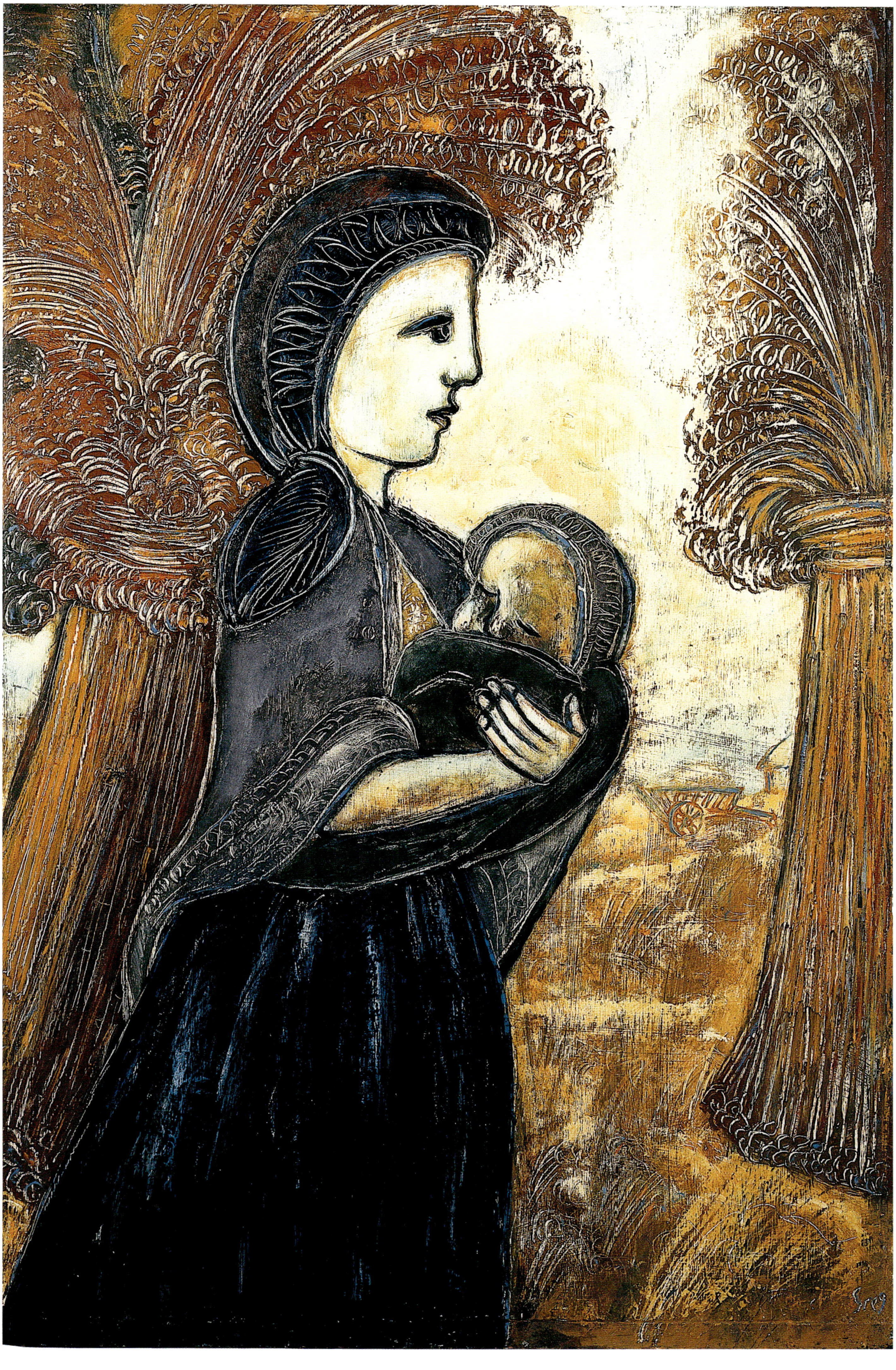

THE WASHING PLACE

FRANÇOIS SOUBIROUS *never gave up hope of finding work and continued to find odd labouring jobs. Louise went to the forest for firewood and to wash clothes in town to earn a little money. There was a village spring at Segus not far from Lourdes, a washing place where the women washed their linen together.*

21¾ x 25¾ inches
Charcoal and acrylic on canvas

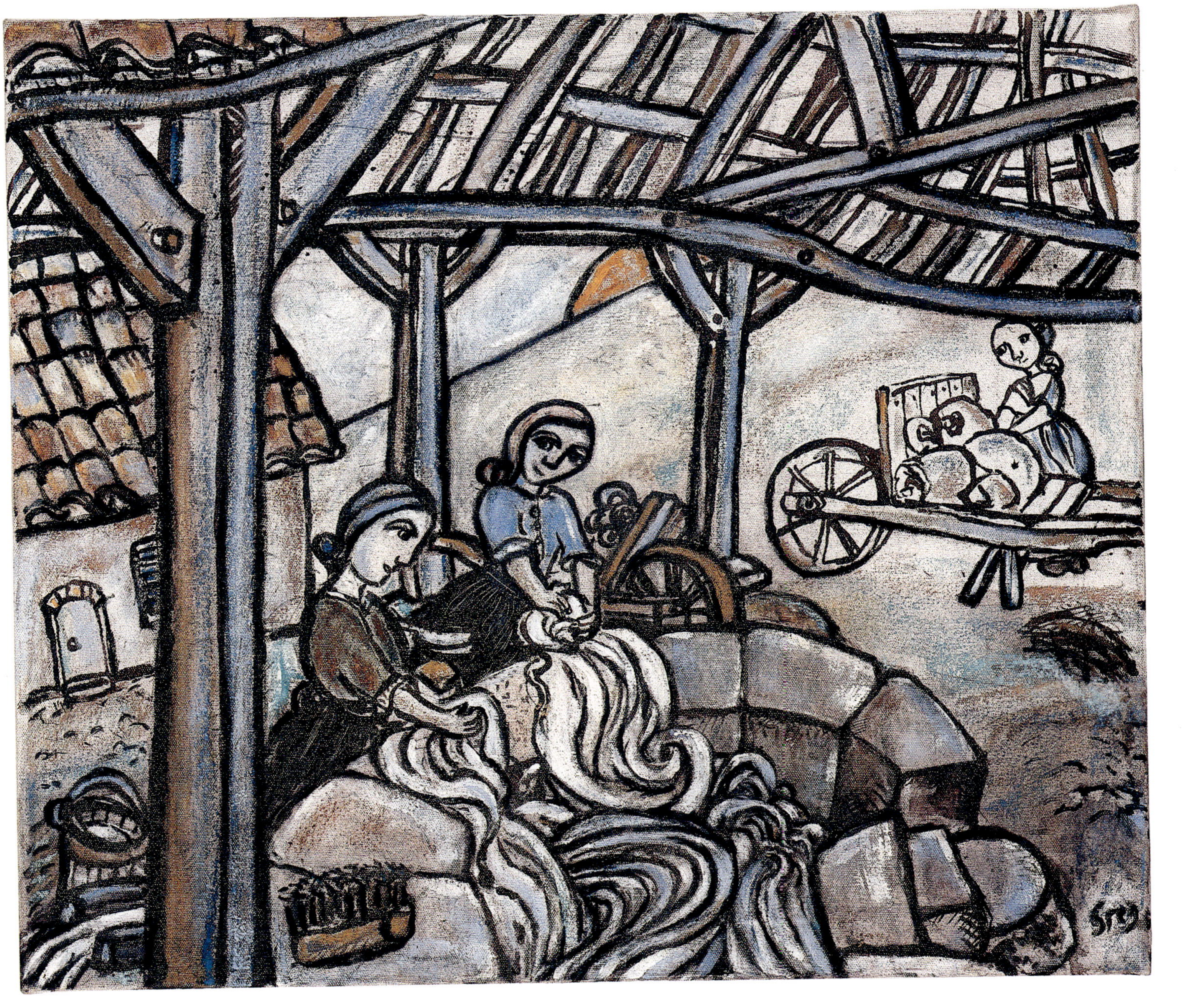

BERNADETTE BY THE FIRESIDE

12¼ x 15¾ inches
Gouache and ink on paper

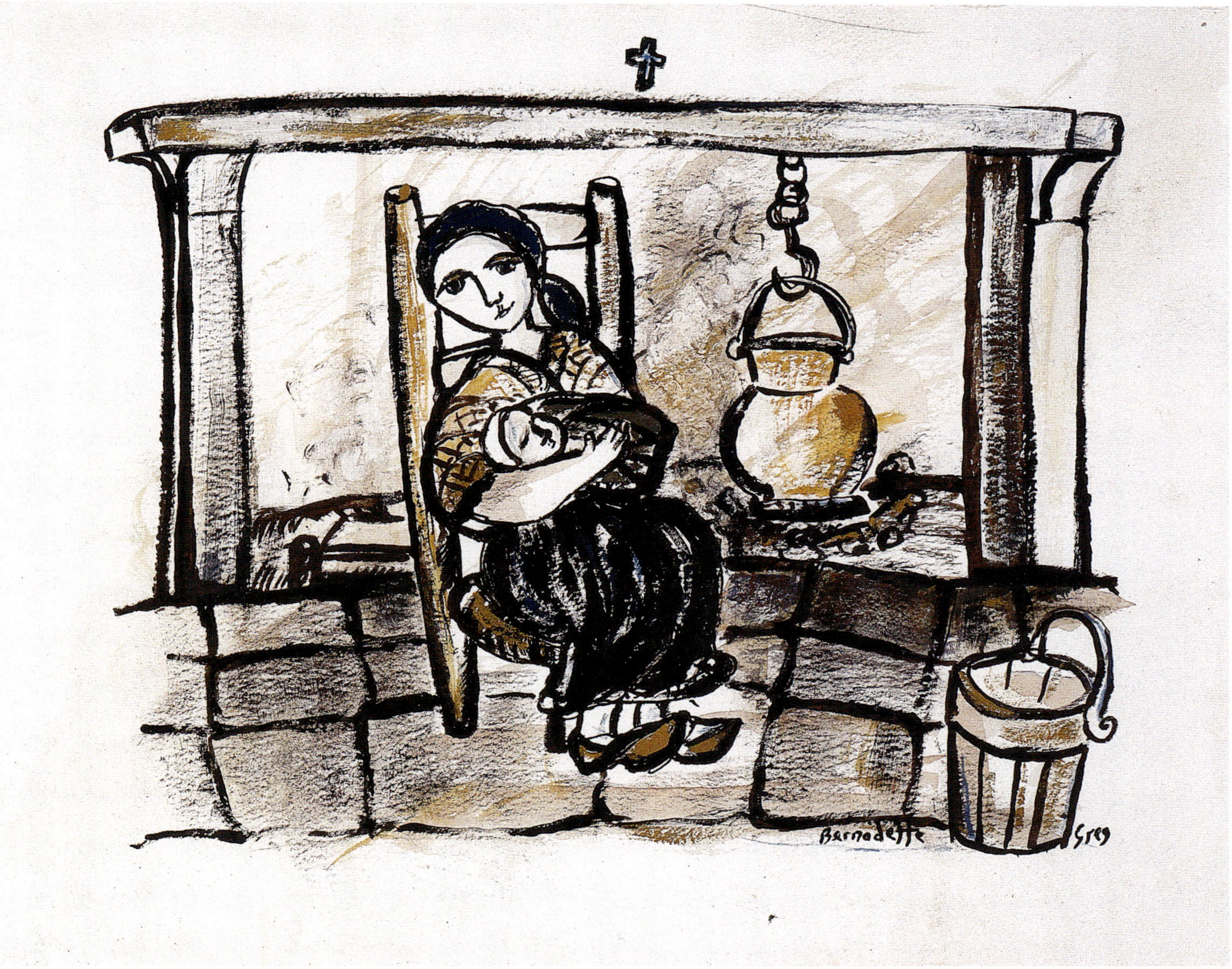
Bernadette

JOURNEY TO LE CACHOT

ON *the move again, the Soubirous family with their few belongings trundle along the Rue des Petits Fossès by the towering castle. The hand cart grinds to a halt outside the grim prison house Le Cachot, where the local stonemason, André Sajous, agreed to let them rent a room.*

They enter by a massive bolted door that leads down a dark narrow passageway to the small cell-like room that had bars on the window. Louise and her daughters give the place a good spring cleaning before they moved in.

34½ x 39½ inches
Charcoal, pastel, gouache and acrylic on wood

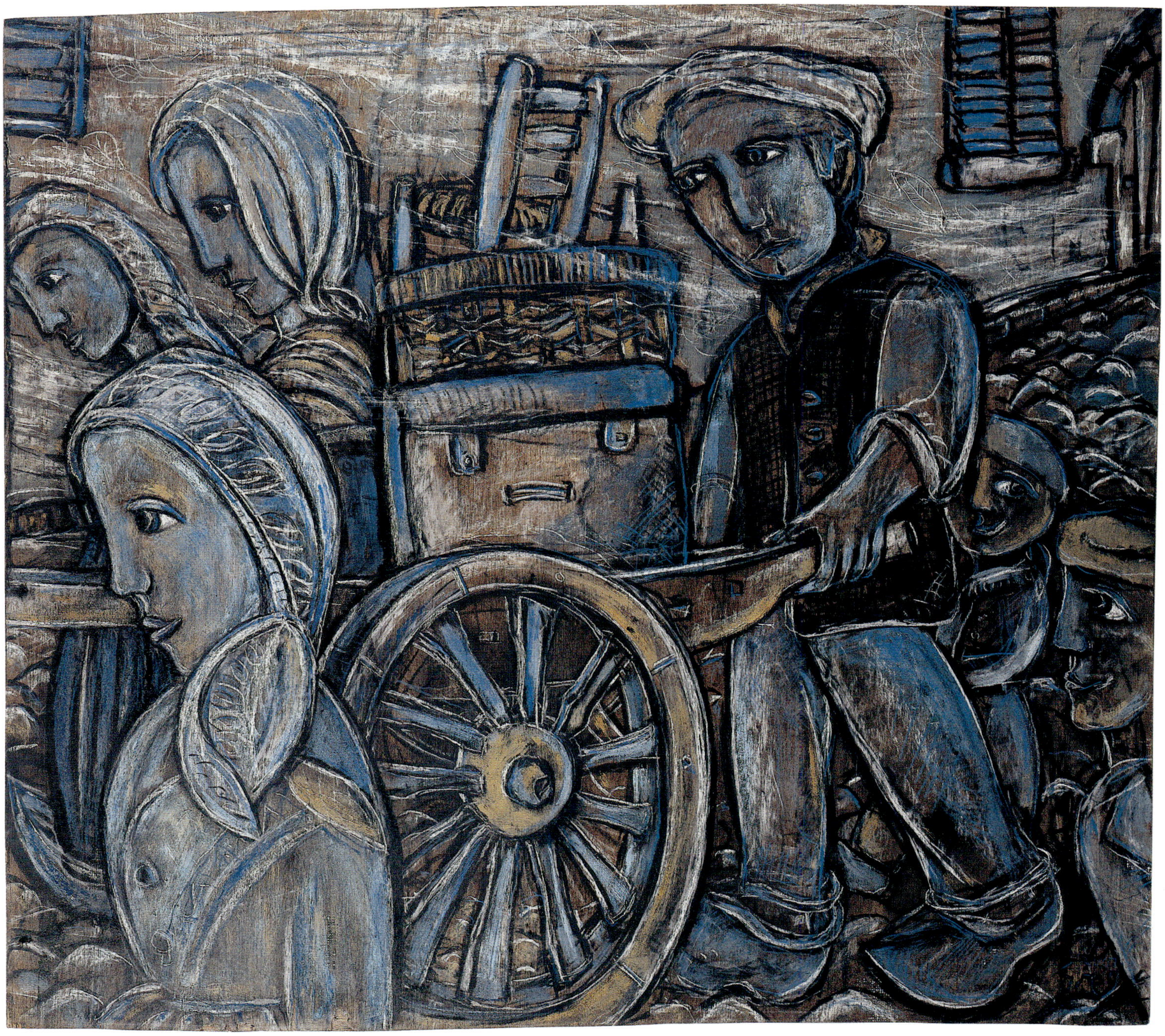

BERNADETTE BY THE WINDOW

IN LE CACHOT, *Bernadette often sat by the window-ledge, with her small bowl of soup, overlooking a blank wall where a dungheap had been left. The bread of the poor was made of a maize dough which upset her stomach. As a treat her mother sometimes managed to give her a little wheat bread and wine.*

"When the good Lord permits it we don't complain.
When we desire nothing we have what we need."

Bernadette

36¾ x 28 inches
Charcoal, acrylic and pastel on wood

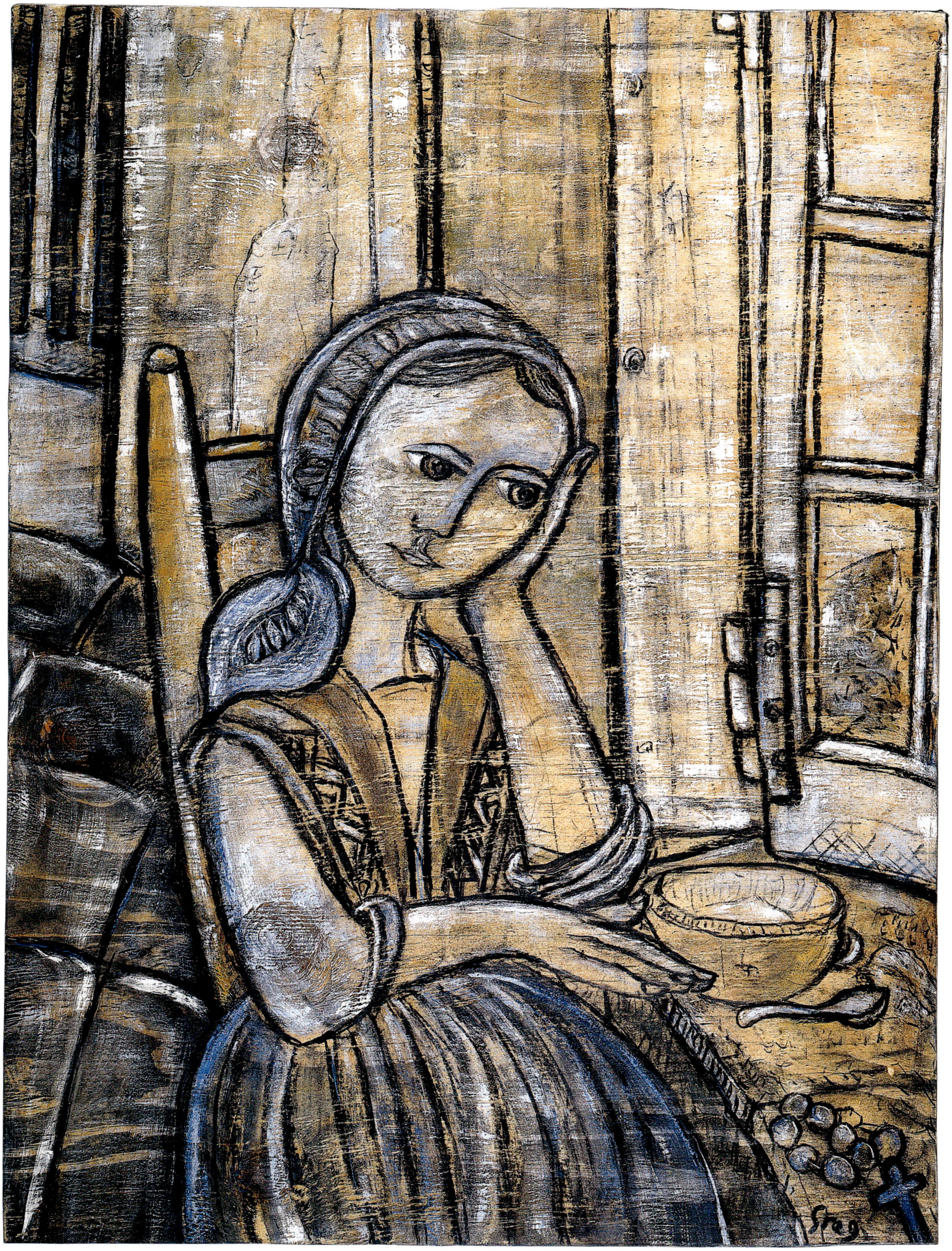

MOTHER & DAUGHTER SEWING

BY *the fireside shadows and the evening light of a resin candle, Louise, with the help of Bernadette, repairs the children's clothes that were wearing out. Louise liked neatness in dress but was unable to achieve as much of it as she would have liked.*

29½ x 33½ inches
Oil on wood

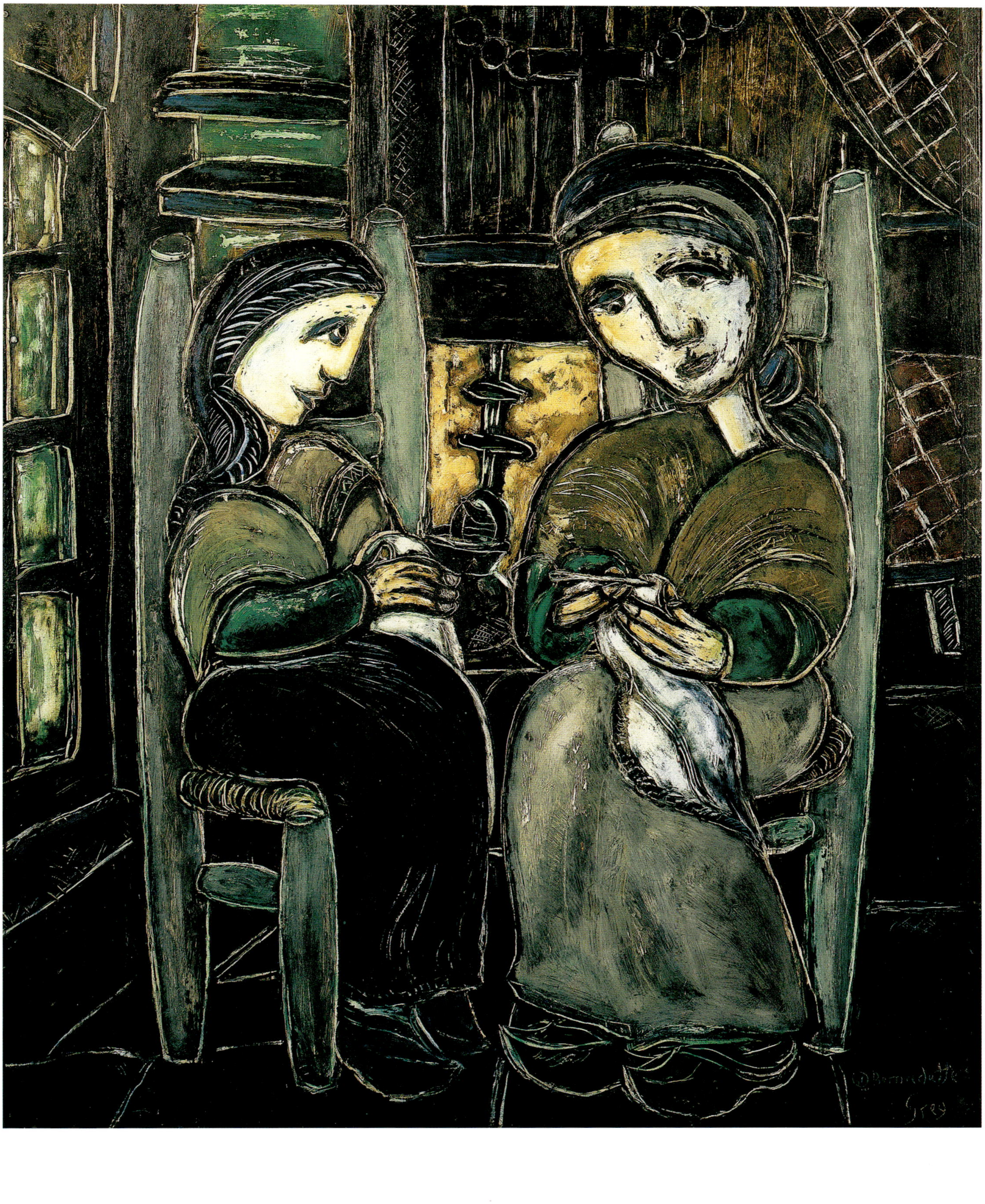

FAMILY PRAYERS IN LE CACHOT

IN *the evening the family gathered together for night prayers. Mother Louise recited aloud the Pater Ave and Credo.*

André Sajous, the stonemason, recalled, "I used to hear them recite their prayers at night. I have no words to describe the fervour with which Bernadette and the others besought their Father in Heaven for their daily bread," and he added: "there were no arguments between François and Louise, never did I hear an ill-natured word from one to another, nor from the children against their parents. Though they corrected their children sternly, as the poor do, they did not ill-treat them."

40½ x 52½ inches
Acrylic, pastel and charcoal on hessian

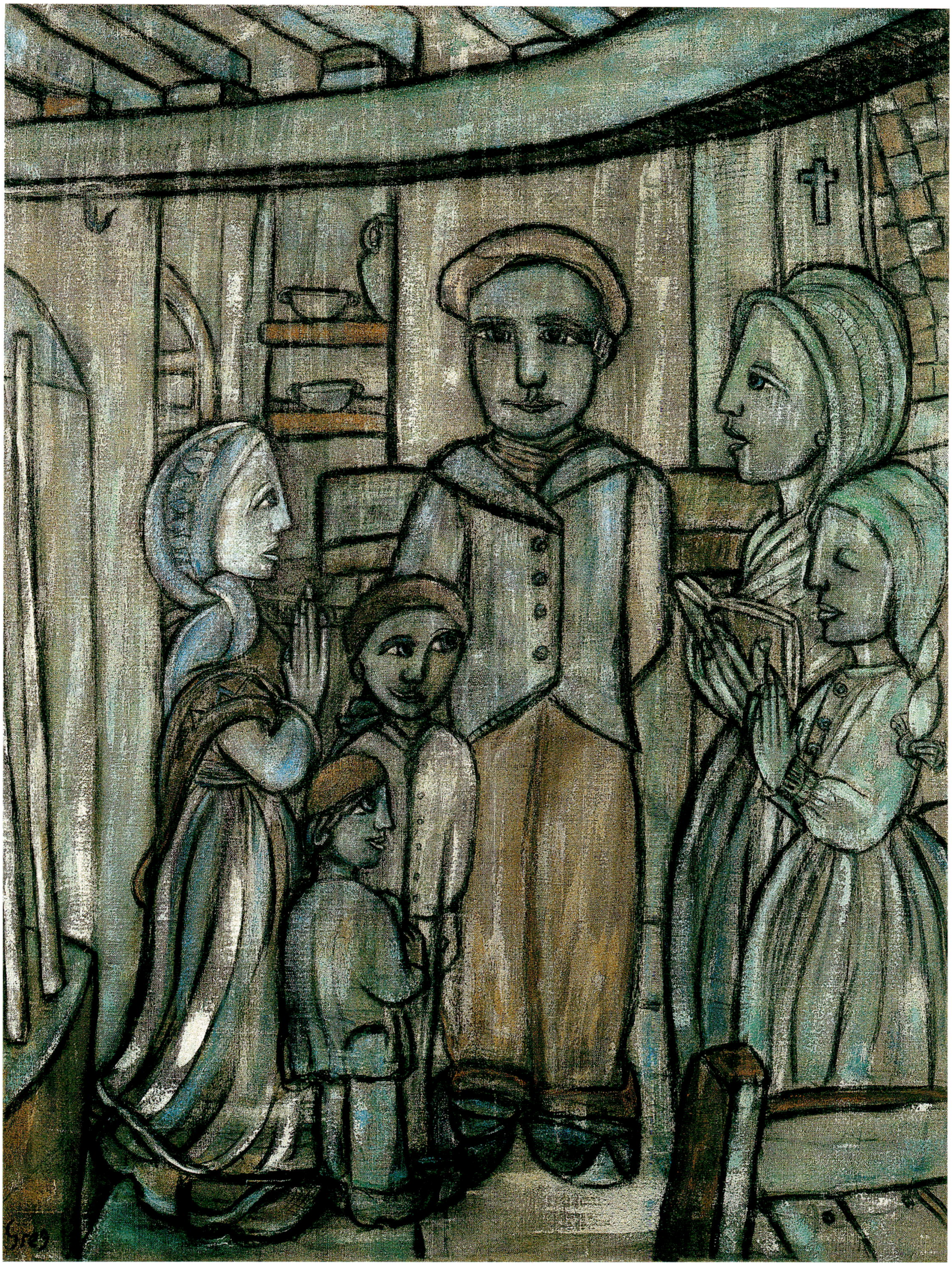

FAMILY PRAYERS IN LE CACHOT - DETAIL

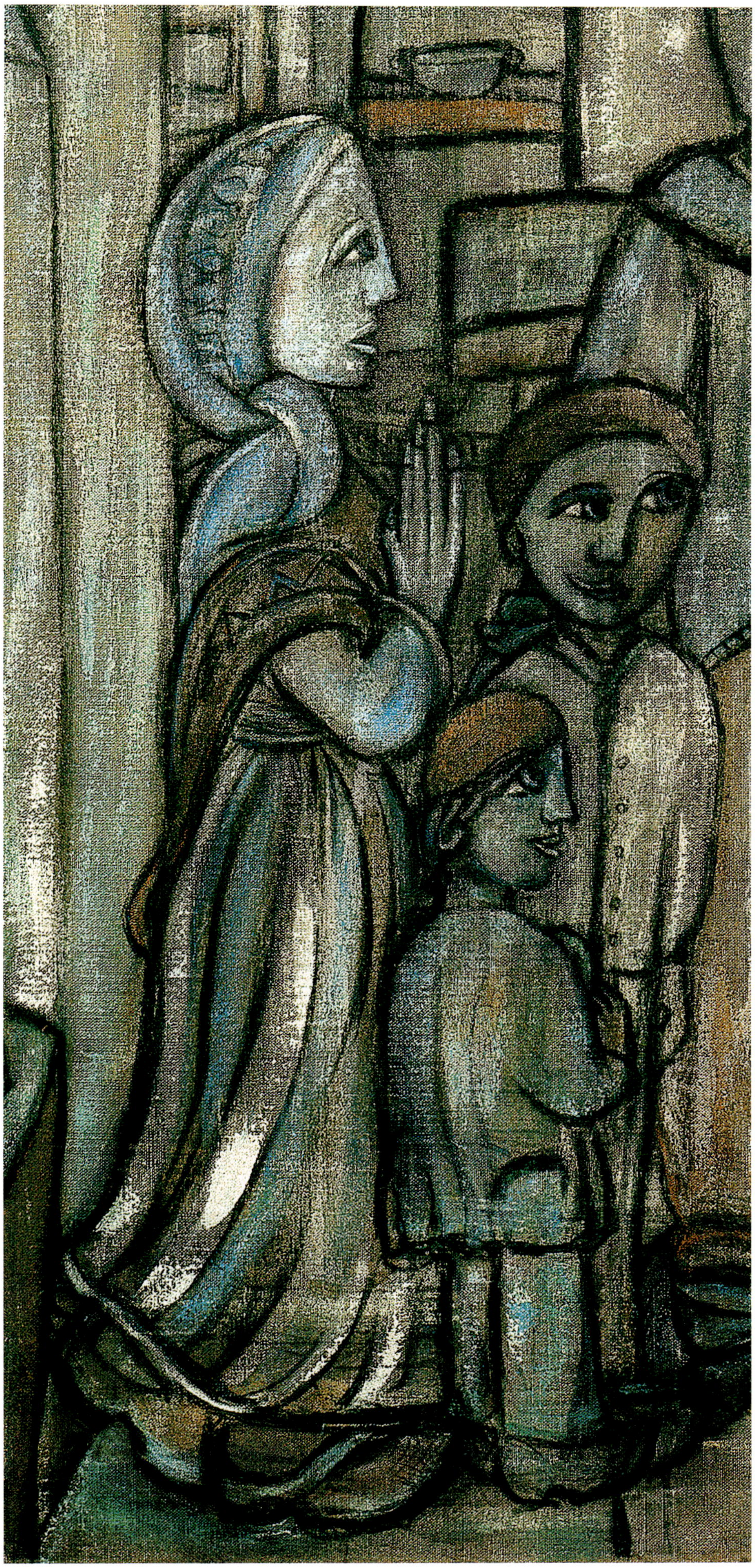

AVE MARIA

In moments of solitude and silence, Bernadette senses a closeness to the spirit of Mary.

73 x 30 inches
Charcoal, pastel and oil on wood

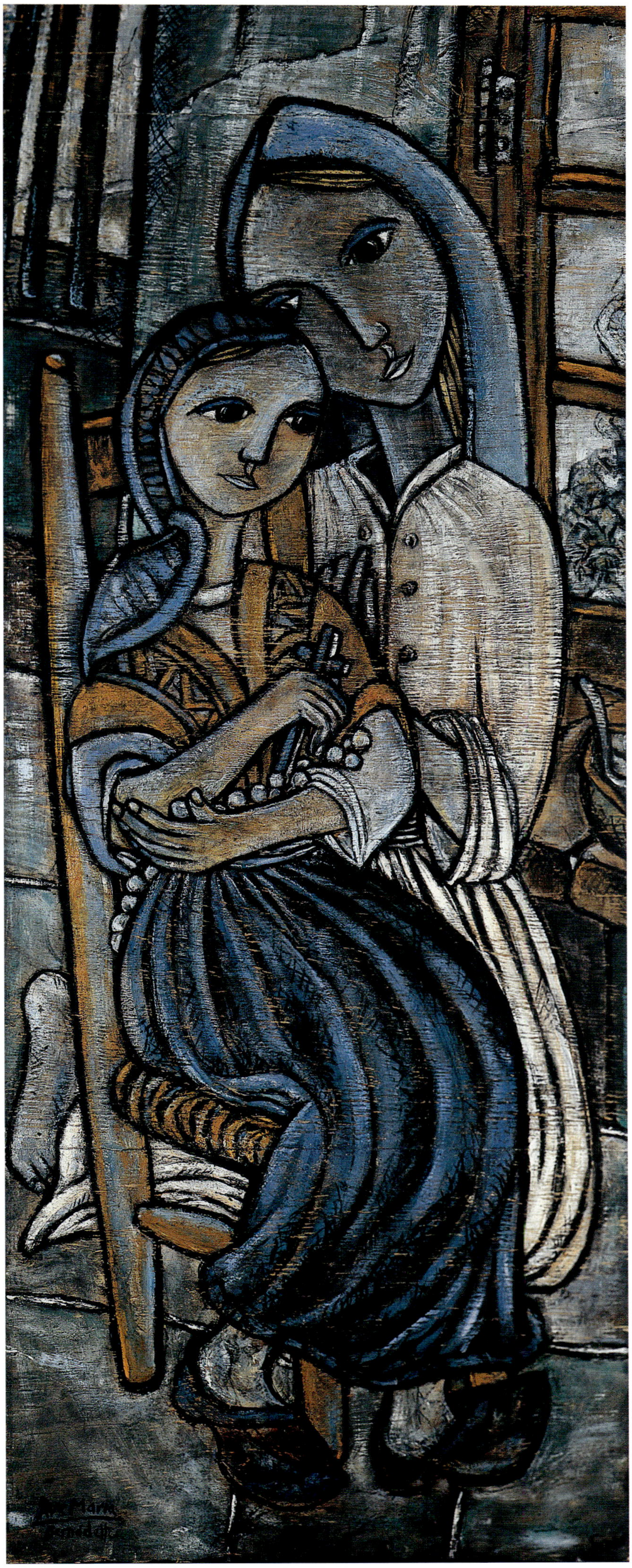

AVE MARIA - DETAIL

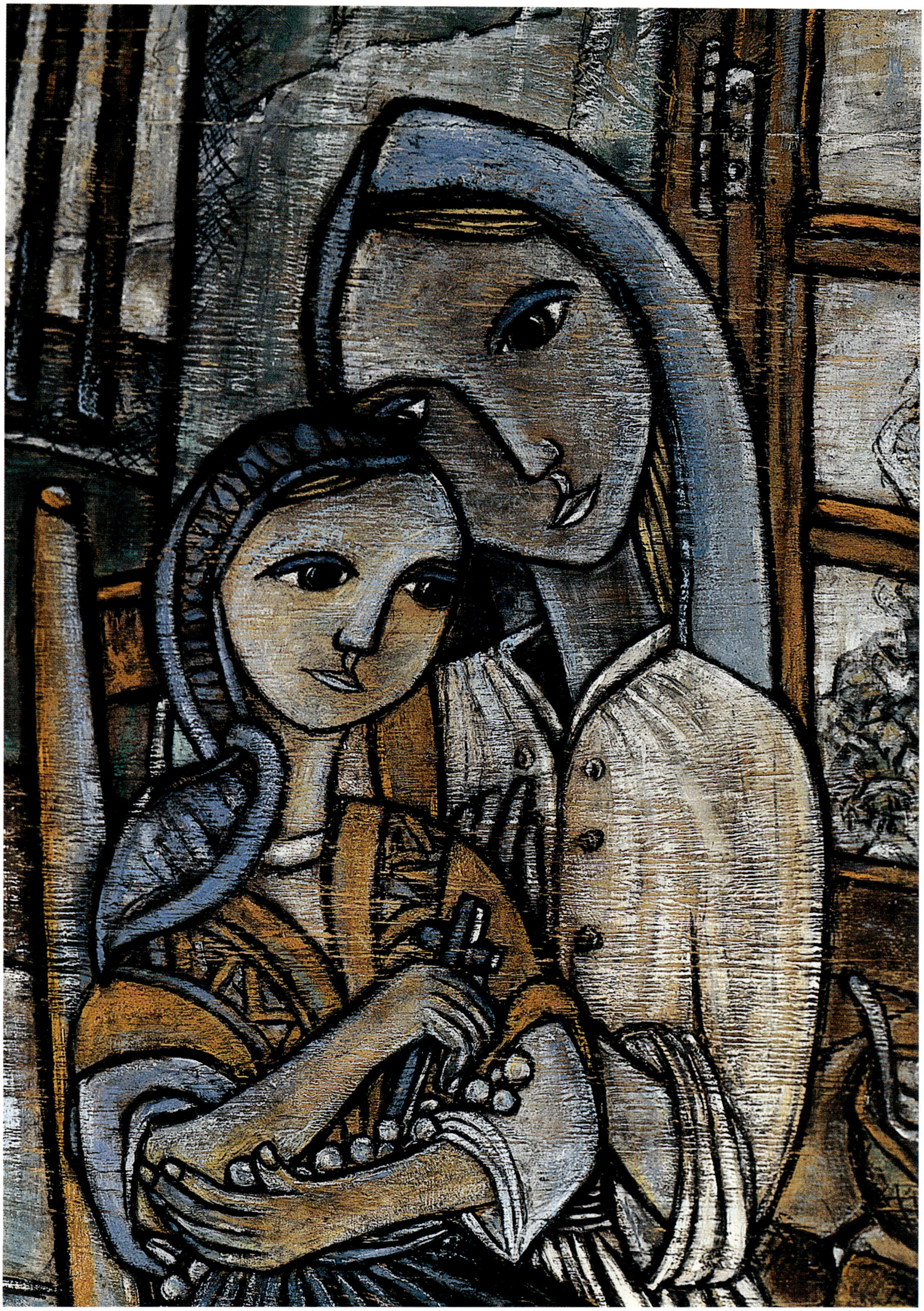

BERNADETTE LOOKS OUT

The heavy bolted door slowly opens. Bernadette looks out; standing at the threshold of life, leaving behind the dark gloomy world of Le Cachot.

23½ x 28¾ inches
Oil on wood

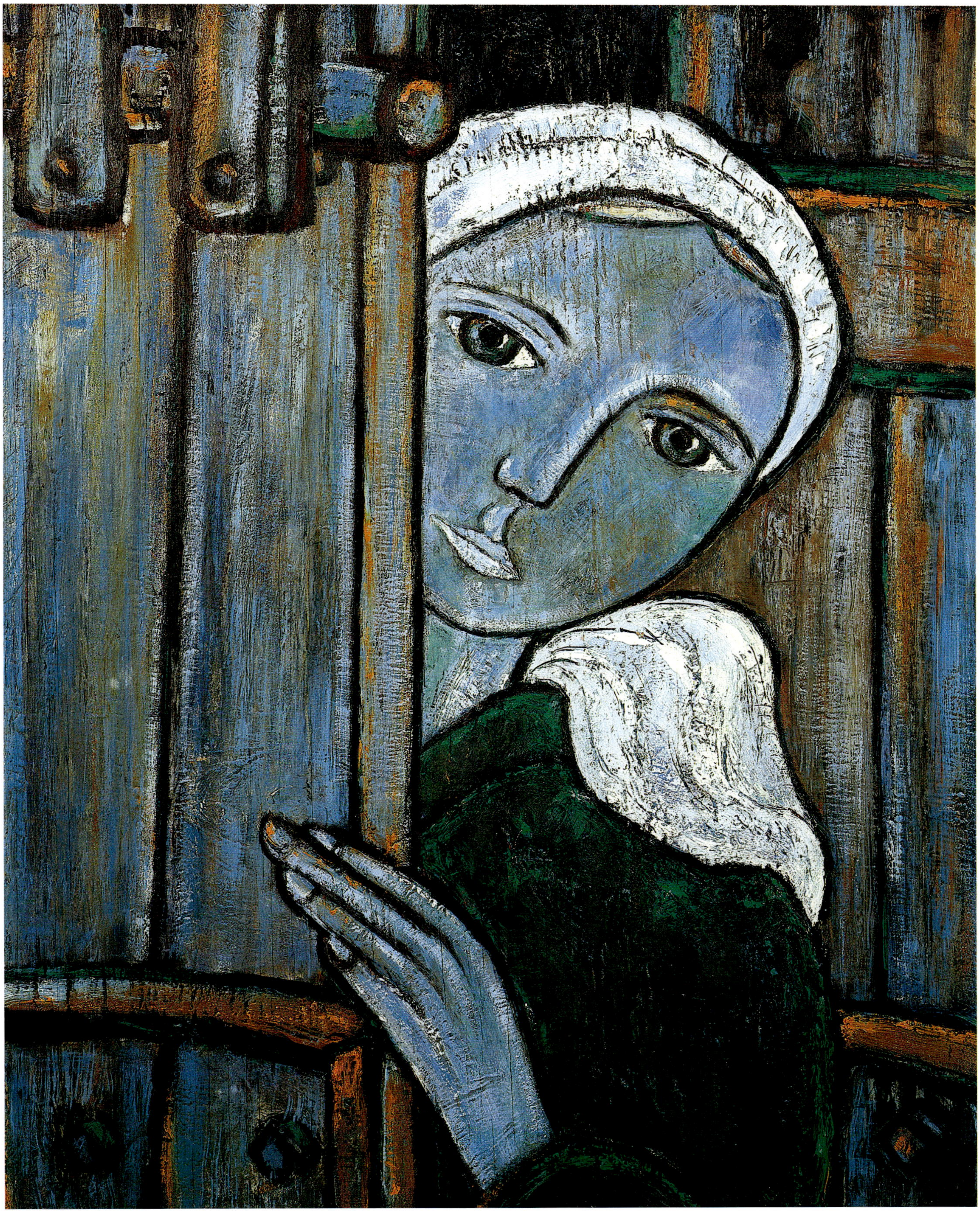

THE KITCHEN AT BARTRÈS

BERNADETTE *was thirteen years old when she returned to Bartrès village to work as a servant girl in the Laguës farm. She stayed in the small servant's room by the kitchen. Years later at Nevers Convent she remained silent about her 'apparitions' and worked humbly with the sisters. Some sisters from Lourdes arrived to see Bernadette and hoped to hear her expound on the 'apparitions', showing her pictures from the grotto. Bernadette abruptly asked them,*

"What do you do with a broom?"
"Well that's a fine question! You use it for sweeping" they answered.
"And afterwards?" Bernadette asked.
"You put it back in its place behind the door."

"And that's my history. The Blessed Virgin used me, then put me back in my place. I'm glad of it and there I stay!"

18 x 16½ inches
Ink, watercolour and pastel on wood

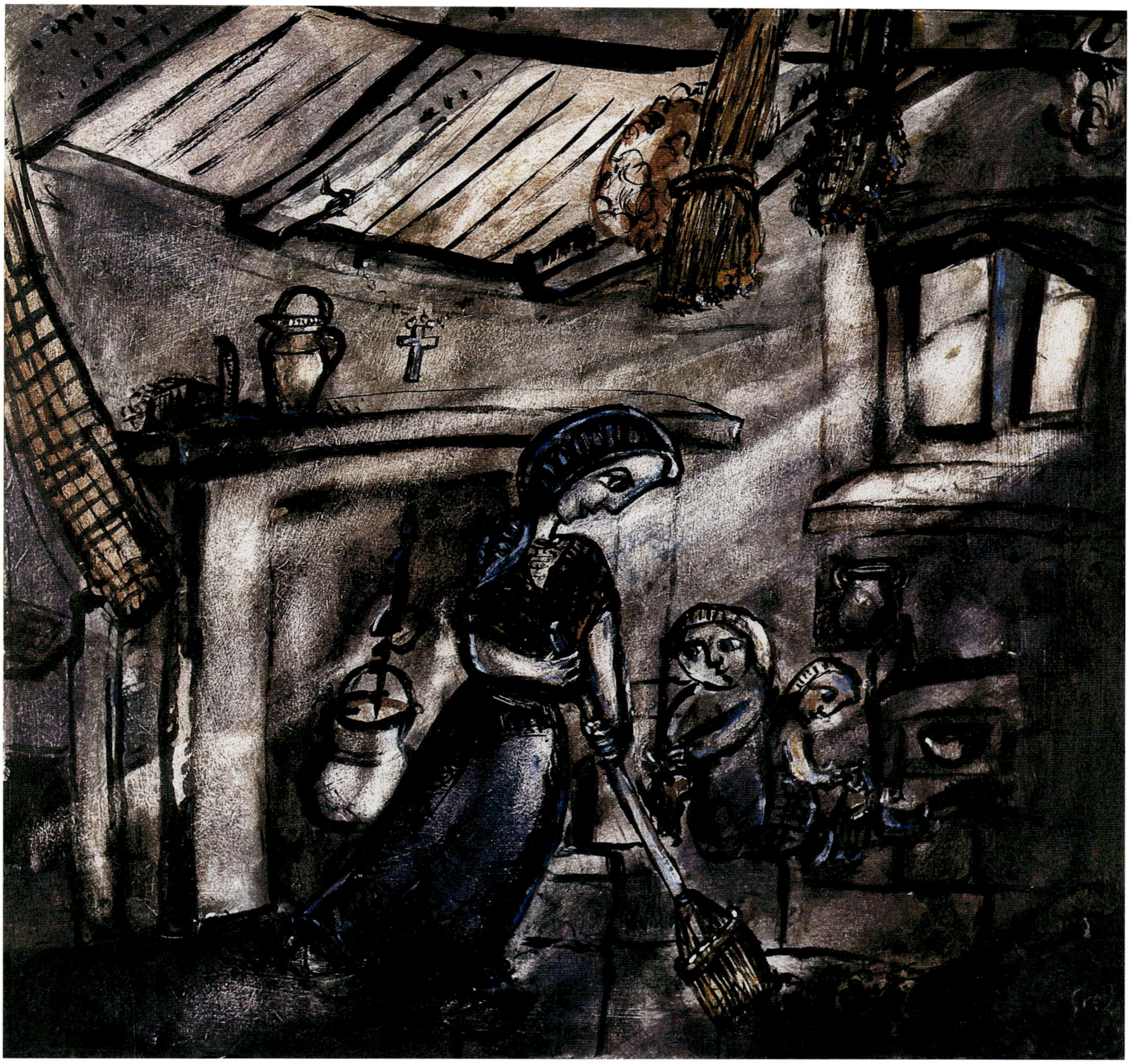

THE SHEPHERDESS RETURNS

THE *chilly wind sweeps down the slopes of Puyono Moor, as the little shepherdess returns. The stream flows along the Bartrès valley to the farm, nestled in the foothills of the Pyrenees.*

72 x 48 inches
Charcoal and acrylic on hessian

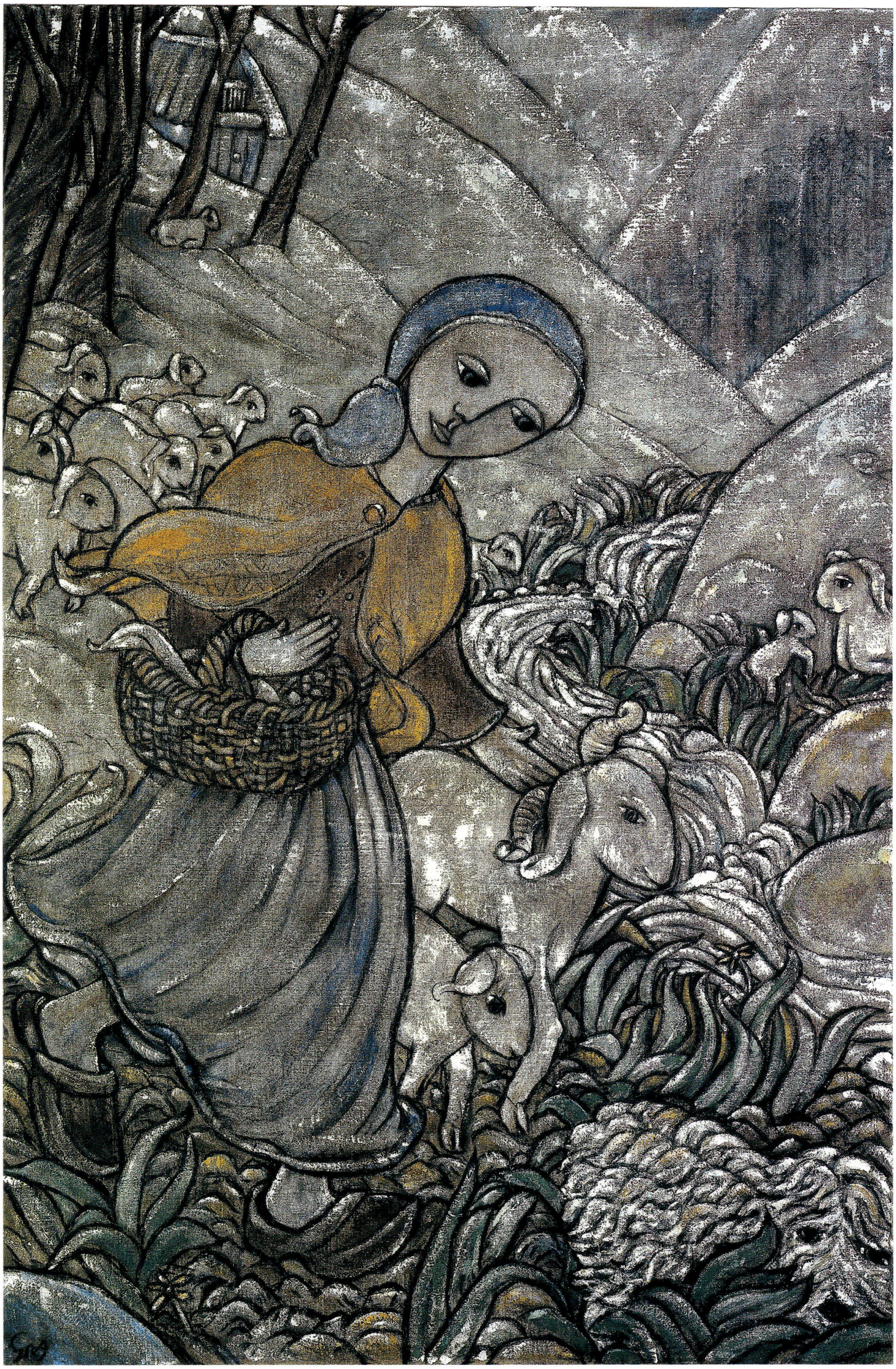

THE VIRGIN STATUE - BARTRÈS

A *legend passed down by an old woman from Bartrès village who spoke in* patois, *the local dialect, said: "that little girl often came to see me. The field where she tended sheep was near to my shed. In the winter, since she was sickly, she came in to warm up. I had a statue of the Virgin on my mantle and Bernadette had fun dressing it up in a little woollen coat which she had knitted herself.*

> *"Why are you doing that?" I asked.*
> *"It's so cold," she answered, "that I don't want the Virgin to be less clothed than I."*
>
> *She always busied herself with my statue. In the summer she wove crowns out of daisies. After the apparitions she came to Bartrès and wanted to see my statue again.*

"Granny," she said to me, "the Virgin from heaven is very beautiful, but I like yours very much because it is the first that I prayed before."

40 x 48½ inches
Acrylic, pastel and charcoal on hessian

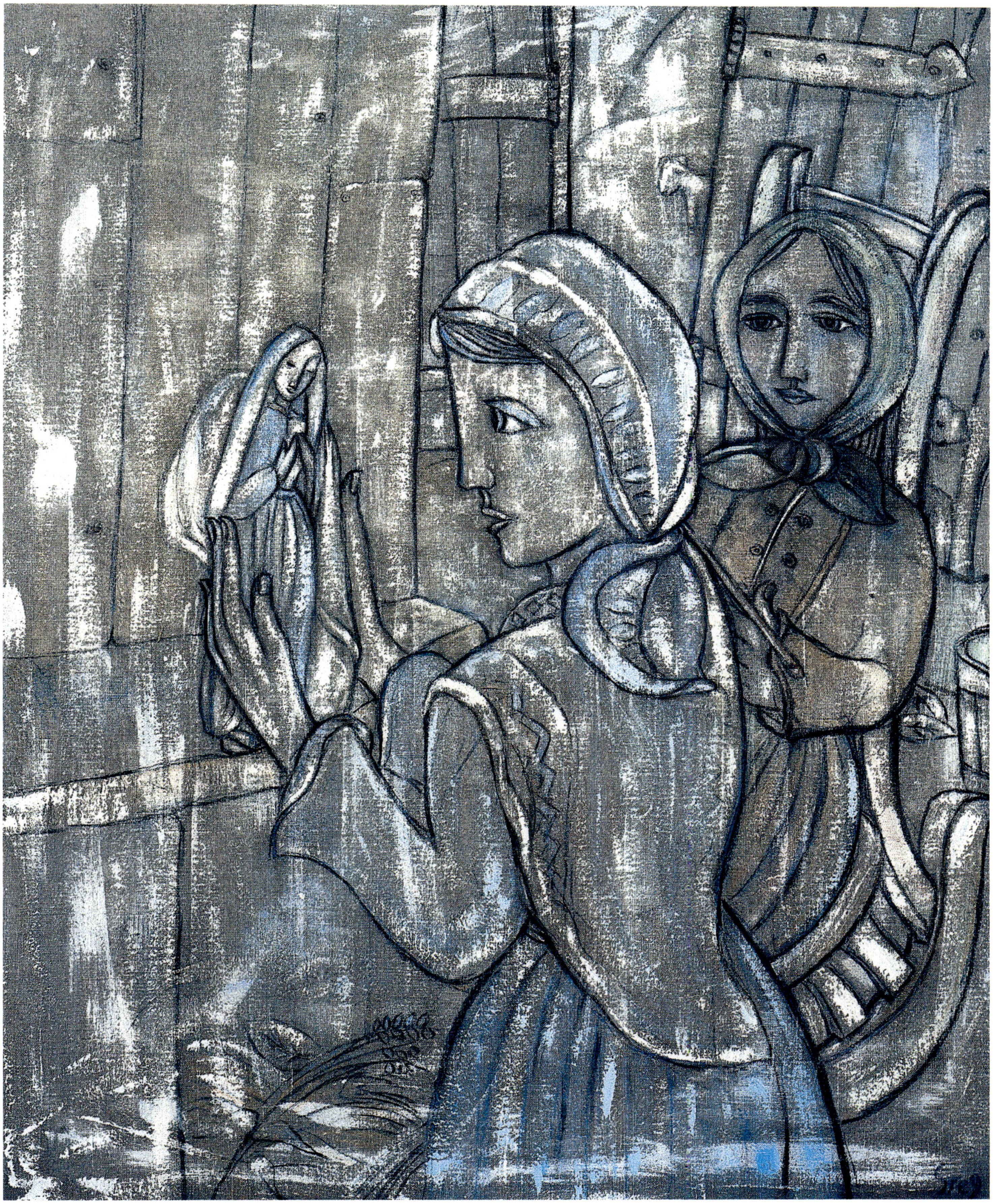

MARIA, SOPHIA

30 x 37½ inches
Oil on canvas

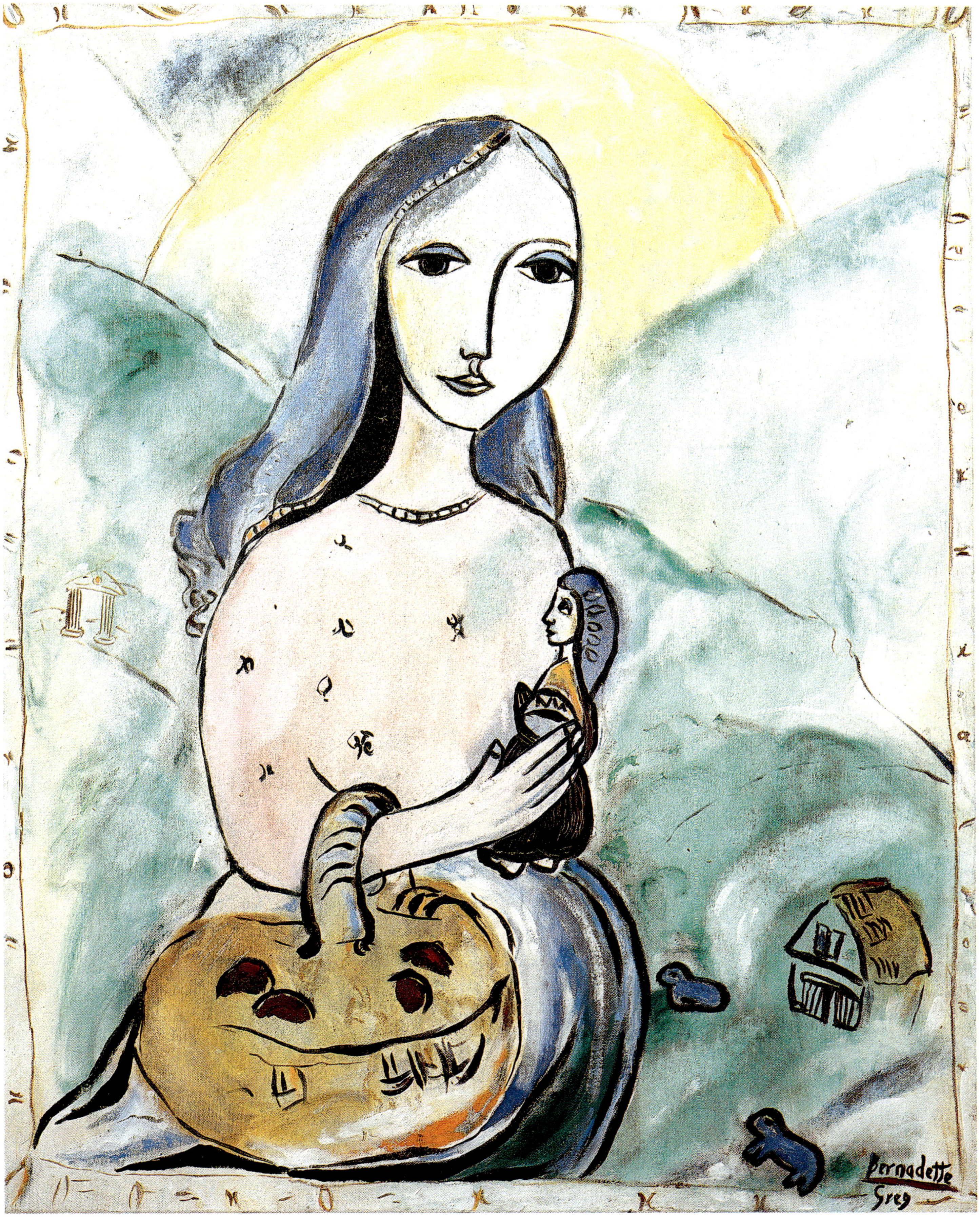
Bernadette
Greg

THE SHEPHERDESS & PIGOU

Blessed are the gentle
As they will inherit the earth
Blessed are the pure in heart
For they will see God

Matthew Chapter 5, V. 5 & 8

19 x 24 inches
Sepia ink and watercolour on wood

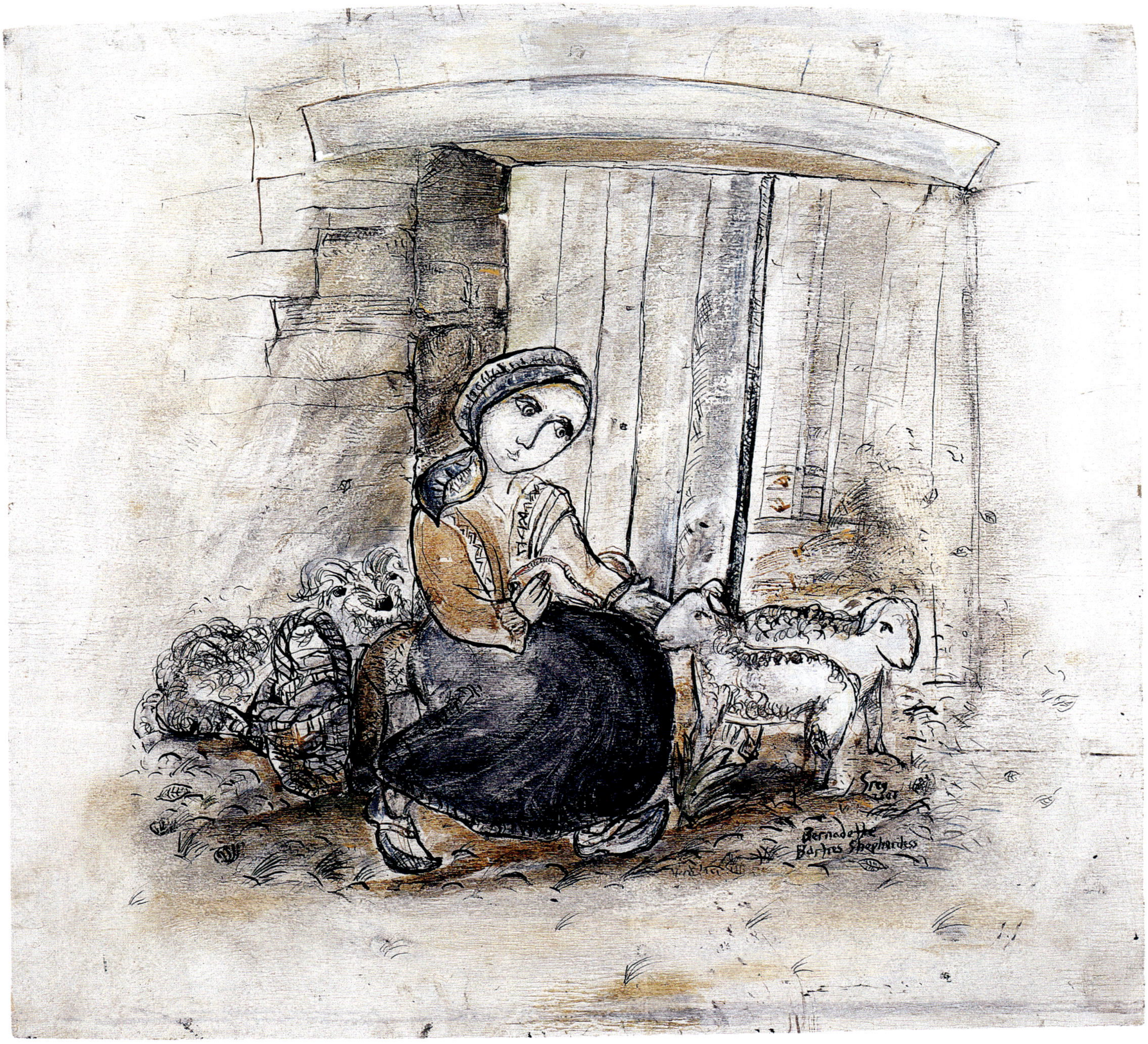
Bernadette
Bartres Shepherdess

THE COURTYARD AT BARTRÈS

BERNADETTE *worked diligently as a servant girl in the farmhouse at Bartrès.*

The family were hardworking people; in the winter evenings the men shelled the maize and repaired the tools, while the women knitted, spun or mended clothes. Later prayers were said in the local patois *before they retired to bed.*

24 x 19 inches
Gouache, ink and pastel on paper

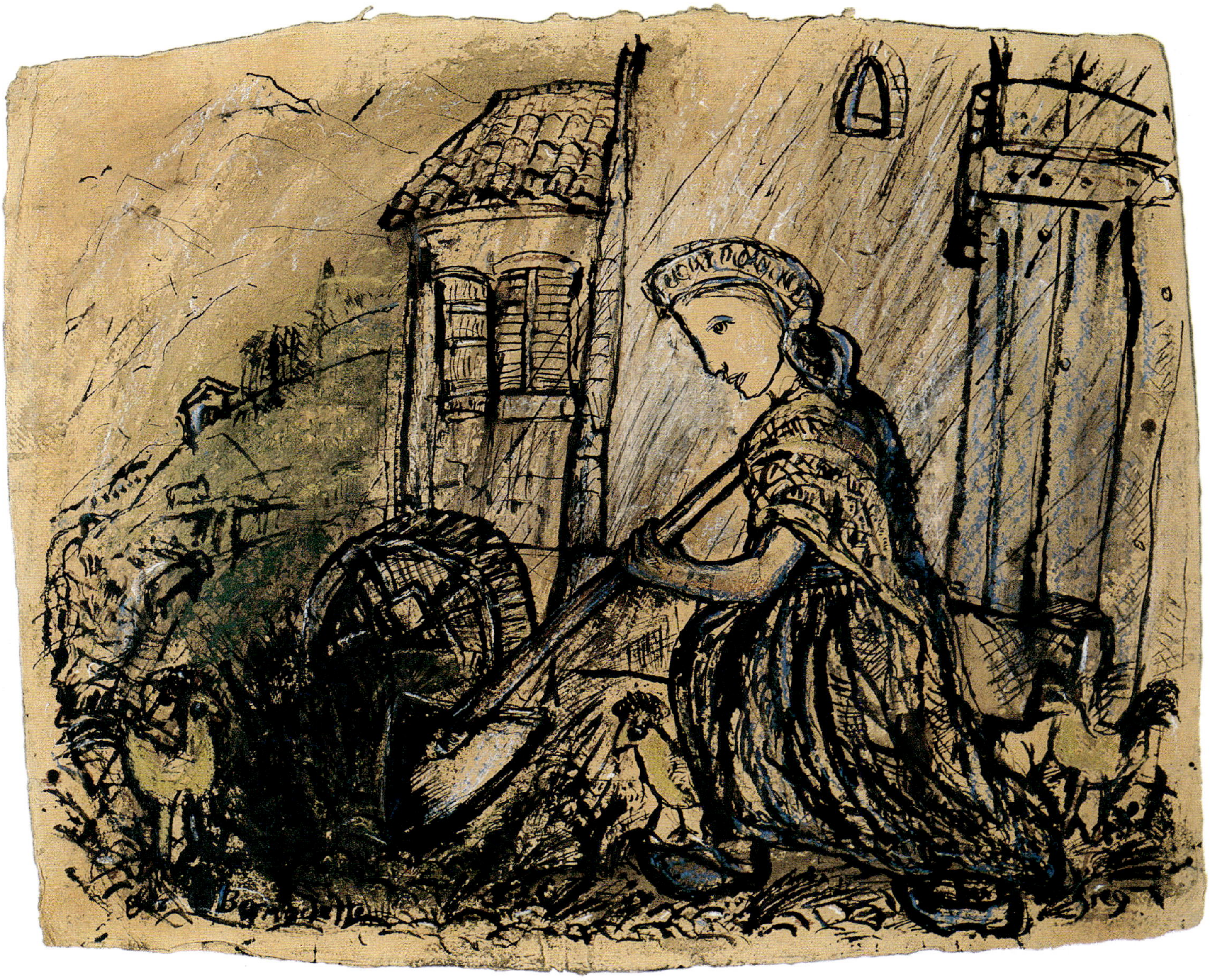

FRANÇOIS IN BED

BERNADETTE *had just turned fourteen when she left Bartrès and returned to Lourdes in January 1858.*

Times were still hard for the Soubirous family at Le Cachot. Paid work for François was scarce. At times he was unable to provide the children with even the food they needed. Then François, leaving for his family what little food there was, would retire to his bed, enduring in silence the pangs of hunger.

25½ x 21¾ inches
Oil on canvas

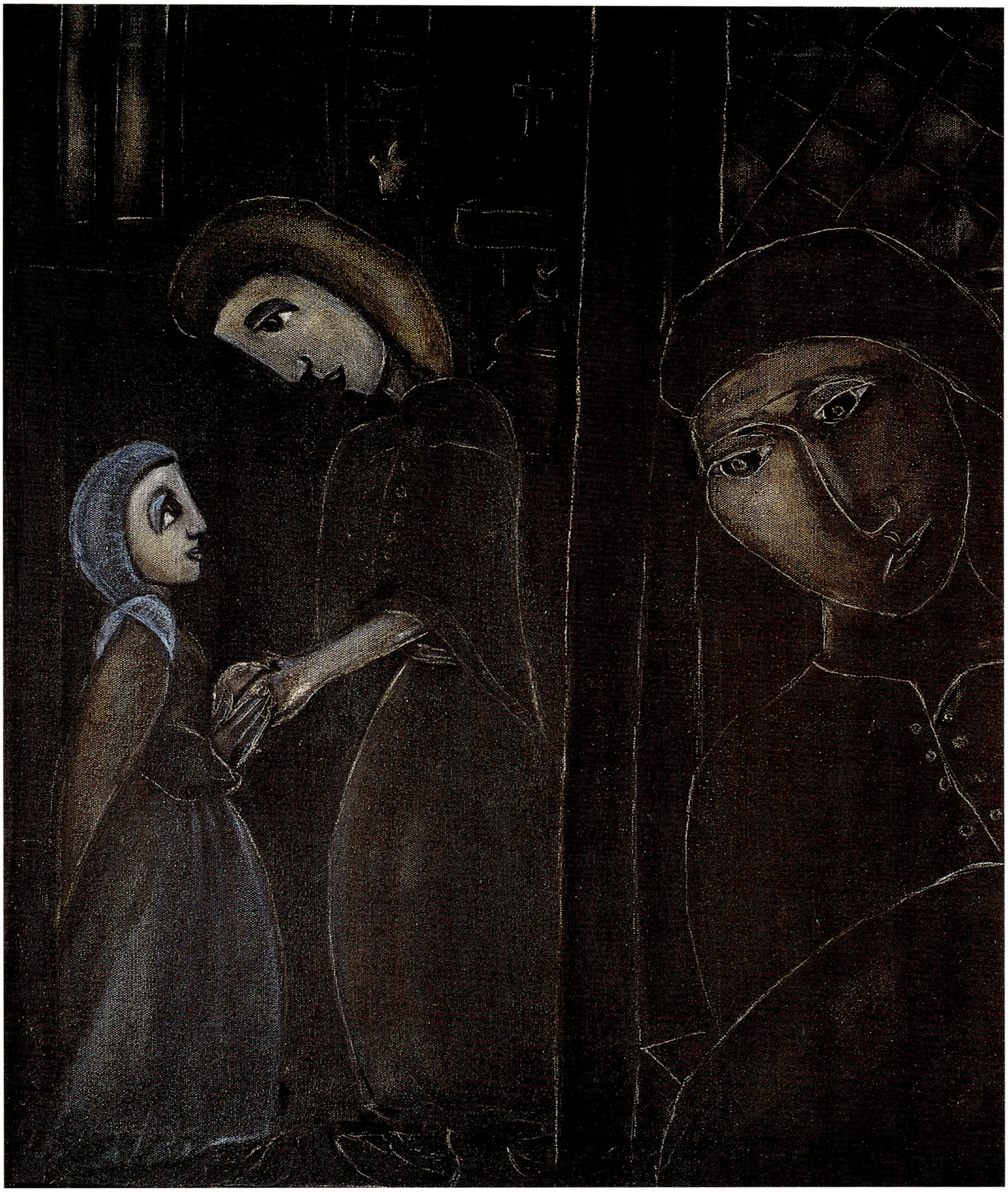

MEETING THE LADY

ON 11th February 1858, leaving Le Cachot, Bernadette, Toinette and a friend, Jeanne, made their way over the wooden bridge that leads past Savy Mill, looking for bones and firewood. A veil of mist shrouded the countryside, town and mountains. The air was cold and damp. At the base of a rocky promontory called 'Massabielle' there was a small stream. The two girls crossed over, leaving Bernadette alone by a boulder. Bernadette recalled her story.

"I had hardly begun to take off my stocking when I heard the sound of wind as in a storm. I turned towards the meadow and I saw that the trees were not moving at all. I had half noticed, but without paying any particular heed, that the branches and brambles were waving beside the grotto. I went on taking my stockings off and was putting one foot into the water when I heard the same sound in front of me. I looked up and saw a cluster of branches and brambles underneath the topmost opening in the grotto, tossing and swaying to and fro, though nothing else stirred all around. Behind these branches and within the opening, I saw immediately afterwards a girl in white, no bigger than myself, who greeted me with a slight bow of the head; at the same time, she stretched out her arms slightly away from her body, opening her hands, as in the pictures of Our Lady; over her right arm hung a rosary."

45 x 29 inches
Acrylic and graphite on wood

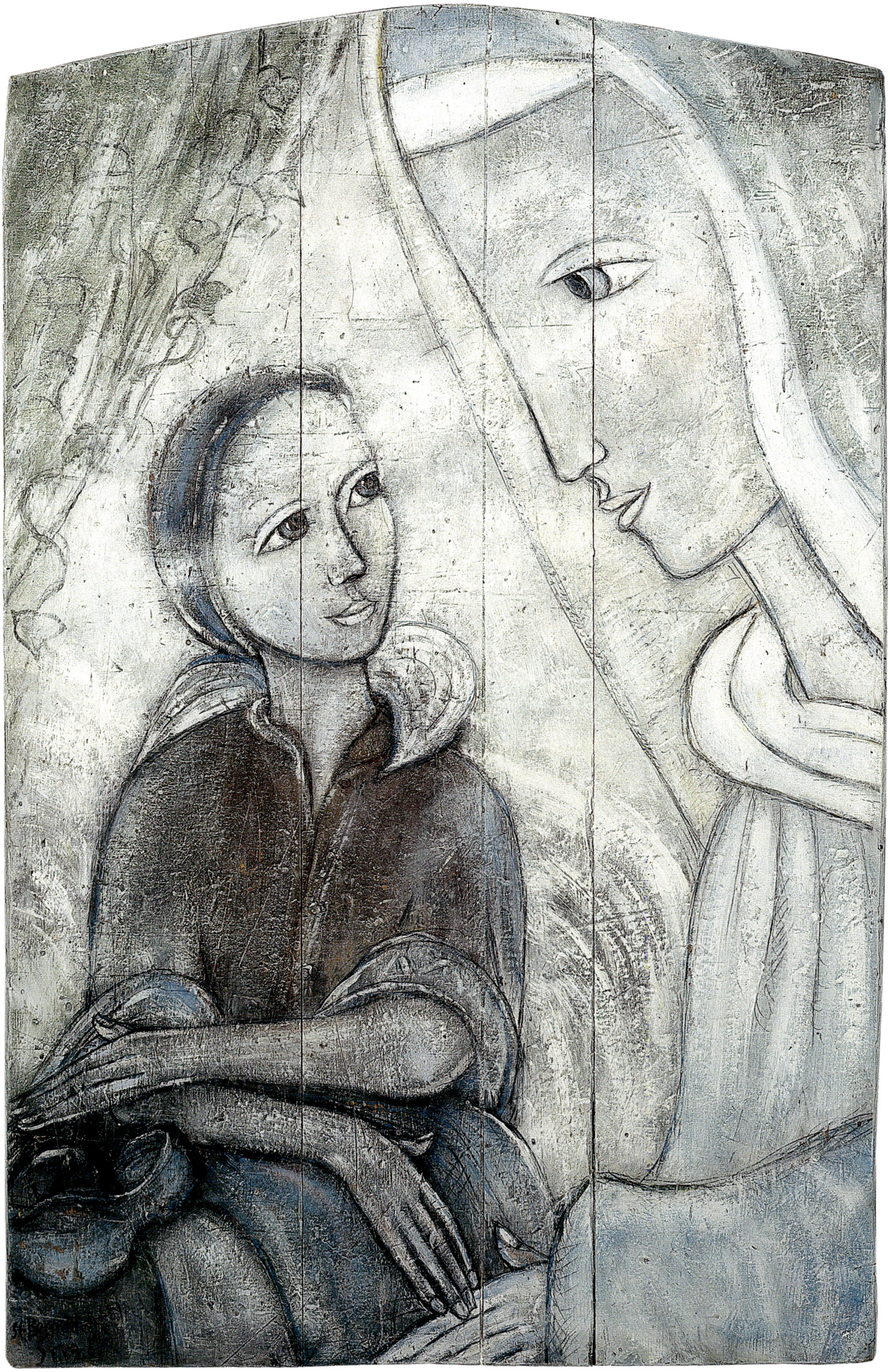

THE HEALING SPRING

BERNADETTE *continued to have a number of apparitions. On the ninth apparition on February 25th there were over three hundred people at Massabielle by the grotto when Bernadette arrived. During her apparition she went back and forth on her knees repeating the word, penance, penance, penance. But then something happened as she recalled, "*Aquerò *(the Lady) told me to drink by the spring and to wash in it. Not seeing any spring, I went to drink at the Gave (river) but she beckoned with her finger for me to go under the rock. I went and found a little muddy water, almost too little for me to hold in the hollow of my hand. Three times I threw it away, it was so dirty. On my fourth try I succeeded." Soon the trickle of water became clearer and continued to flow like a small spring from the mossy rocks.*

31½ x 42½ inches
Oil on wood

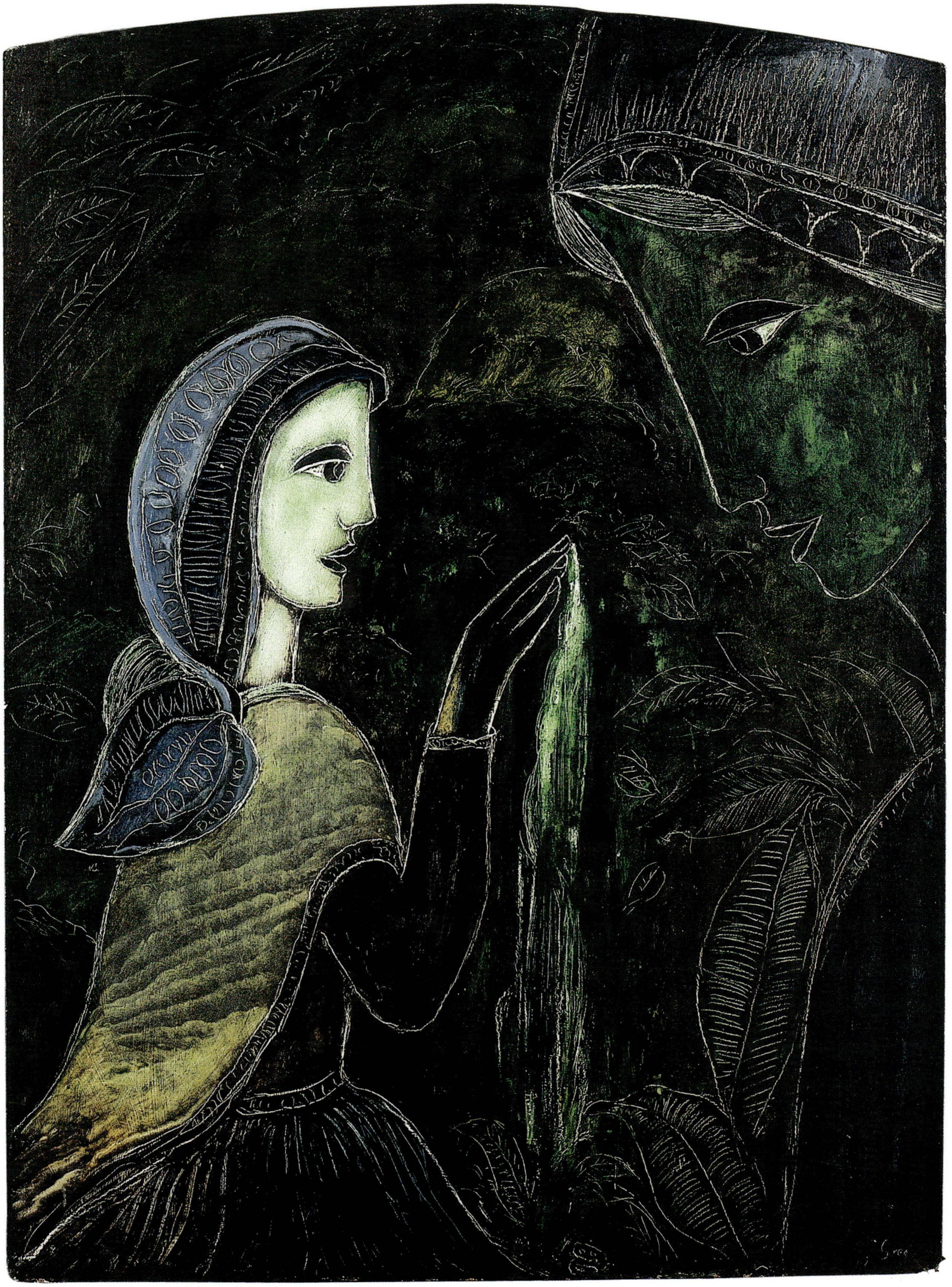

THE HEALING SPRING - DETAIL

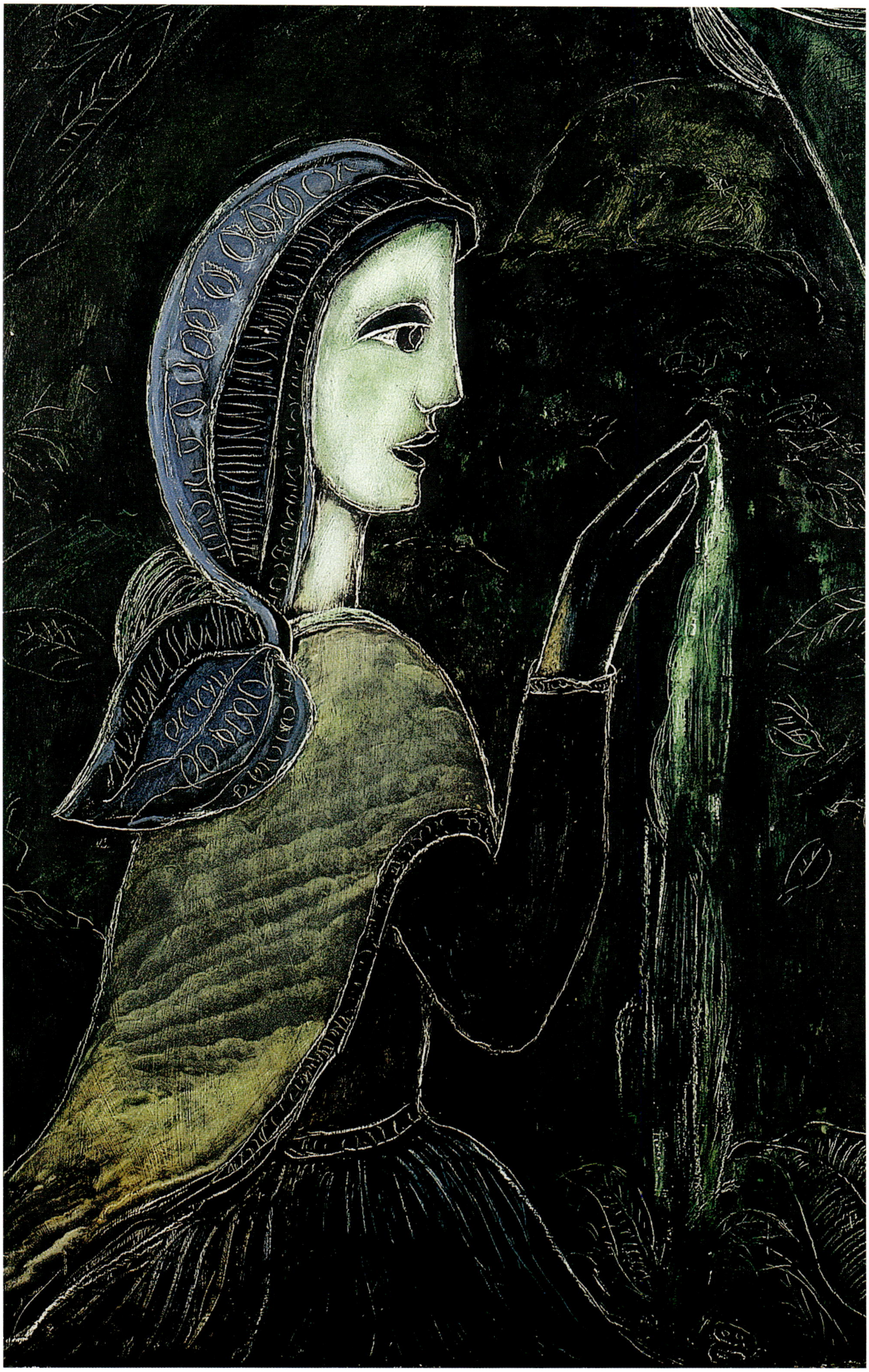

BERNADETTE & THE STONEMASON

THE *presence of Mary speaks through the sacred blues and emerald greens of Chartres Cathedral, ringing out down through the ages. As if bathed in the sacred light, Bernadette looks around the rough-hewn planks at the timeless ancient craft of the stonemason. The workshop of André Sajous, the stonemason, was adjacent to the Soubirous family home in Le Cachot.*

47¾ x 33 inches
Oil on wood

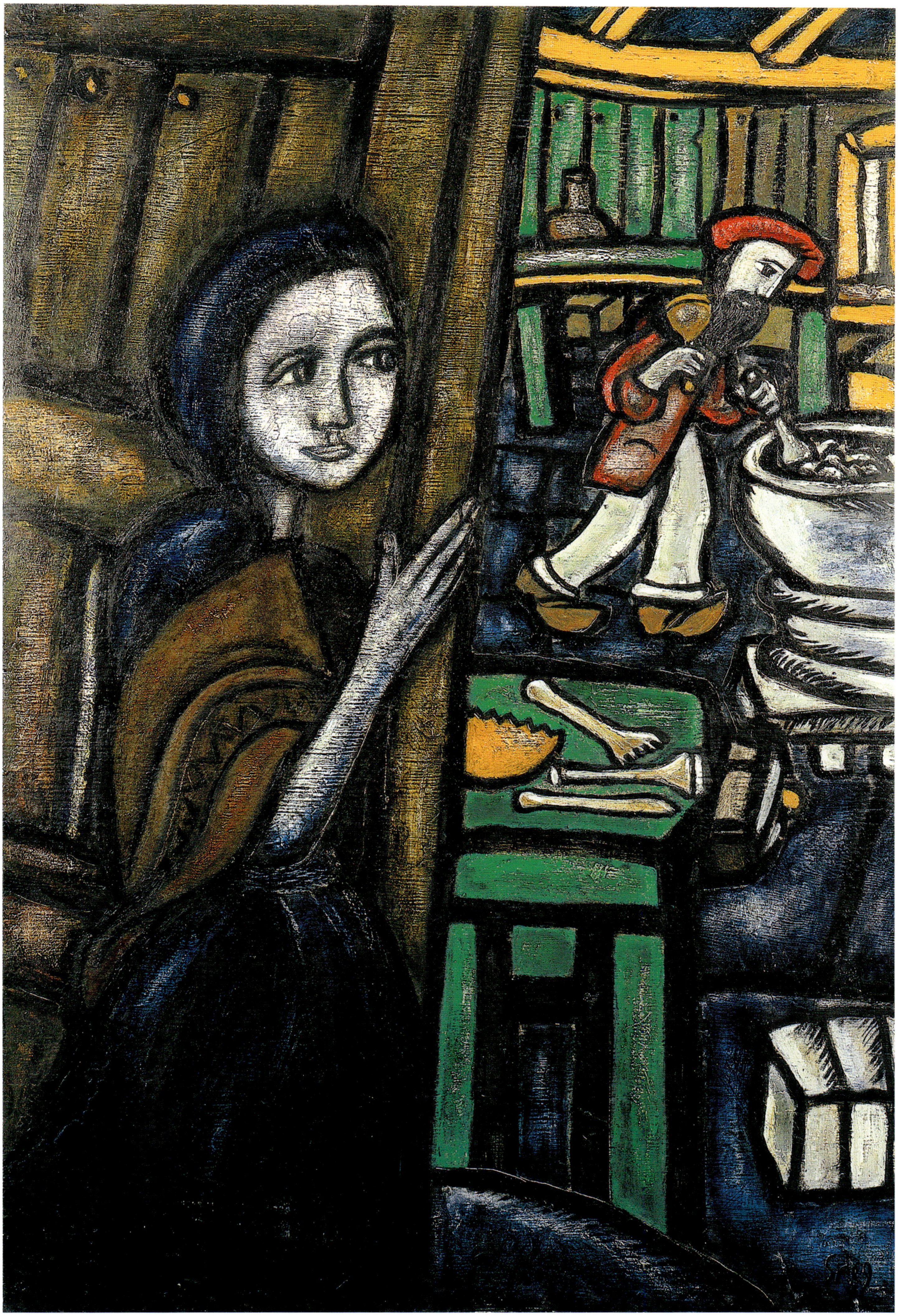

THE BLIND GIRL

On March 4th, the day of the fifteenth apparition, Bernadette silently made her way to the River Gave. On the way a man from Luz approached her and begged: "Pray for my child who is blind." The little child was wearing a hooded cape, in the regional red of her valley. She was frail and had a bandage covering her eyes.

Bernadette looked at her and said to the man, "go make her wash in the spring." At the grotto the press of the crowd was very great around Bernadette. Later, after the apparition, Bernadette climbed the hill and made her way through the crowds around her. Through a small opening in the crowd she could see the girl in the red hood. Bernadette looked upon the unhappy girl with affection. The girl wore the bandage to conceal the state of her diseased eyelids and to shield them from the light. She was often made fun of at school. Bernadette came before her; she took her hands and gave her a kiss. The little girl felt reborn and both girls burst out laughing, holding each other's hands. The girl, Eugénie from Barèges, was soon filled with a warm sense of blessing. She didn't suffer anymore.

17 x 17¼ inches
Charcoal and acrylic on wood

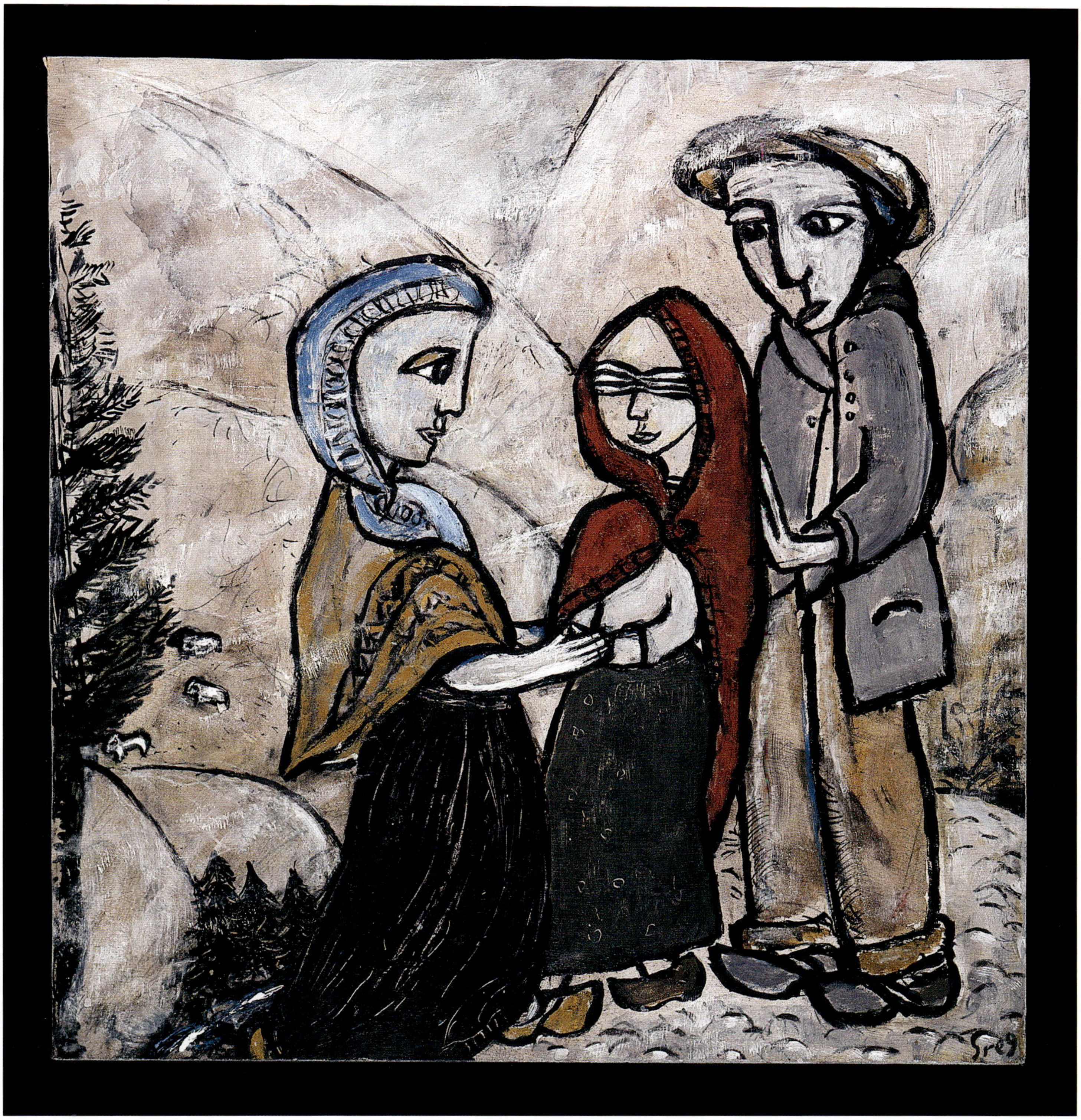

WAITING TO SEE BERNADETTE

OUTSIDE *Le Cachot, crowds of people were waiting to see Bernadette and to have their rosaries touched by her. Bernadette's humble 'two cent' rosary was coveted by many who would have traded their beautifully wrought gold ones for hers. But Bernadette would neither receive or exchange anything. In contrast to the poverty of Le Cachot, rich people waited in line with hoopskirts, jewels and shiny hats.*

20¼ x 17 inches
Gouache, pastel and charcoal on wood

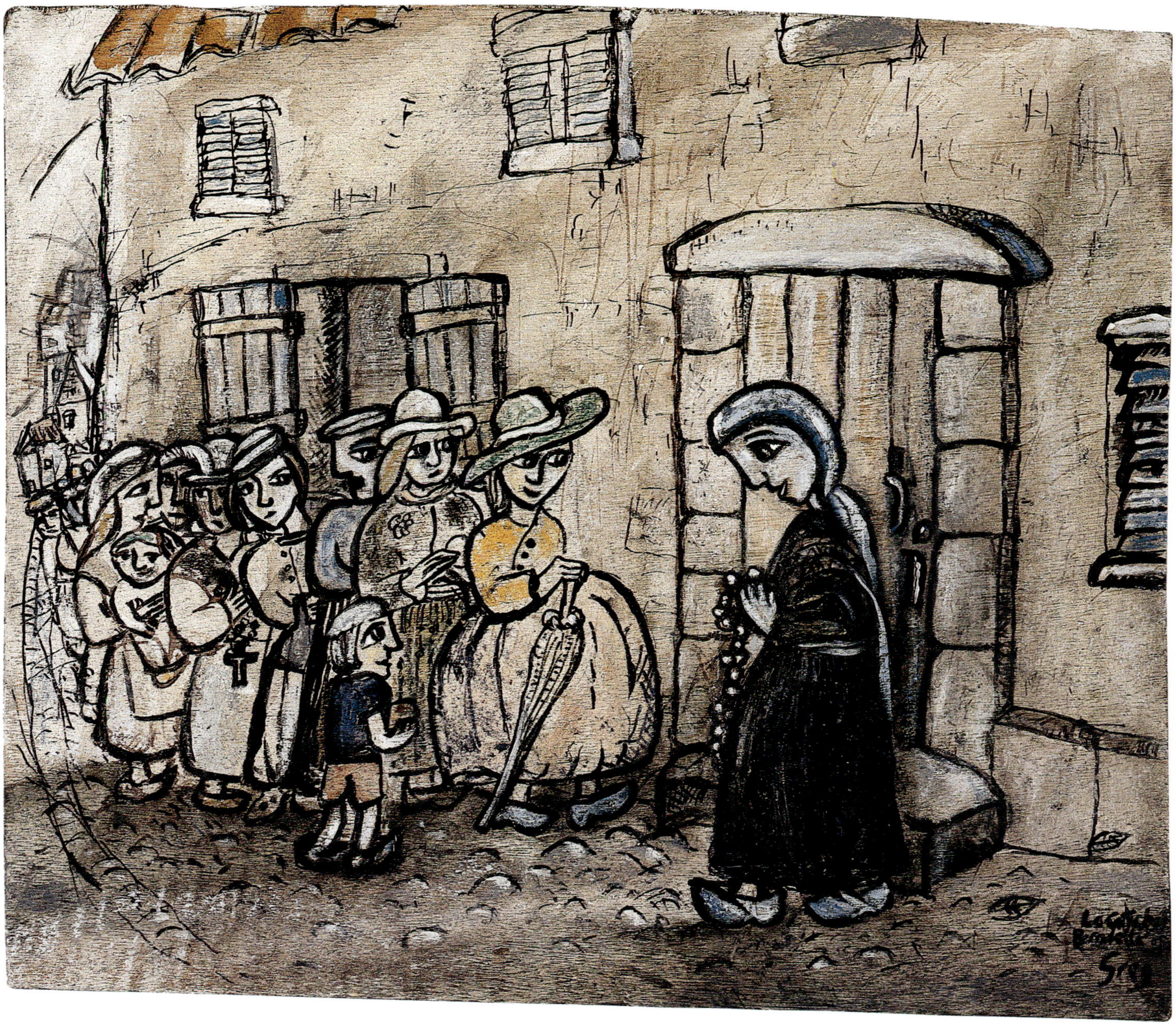

MOTHER MARY

Blessed are the poor in spirit for theirs is the kingdom of heaven.
Blessed are the meek for they shall possess the earth.

Matthew 5 V. 3, 4.

40¼ x 33¼ inches
Oil, gold leaf and charcoal on wood

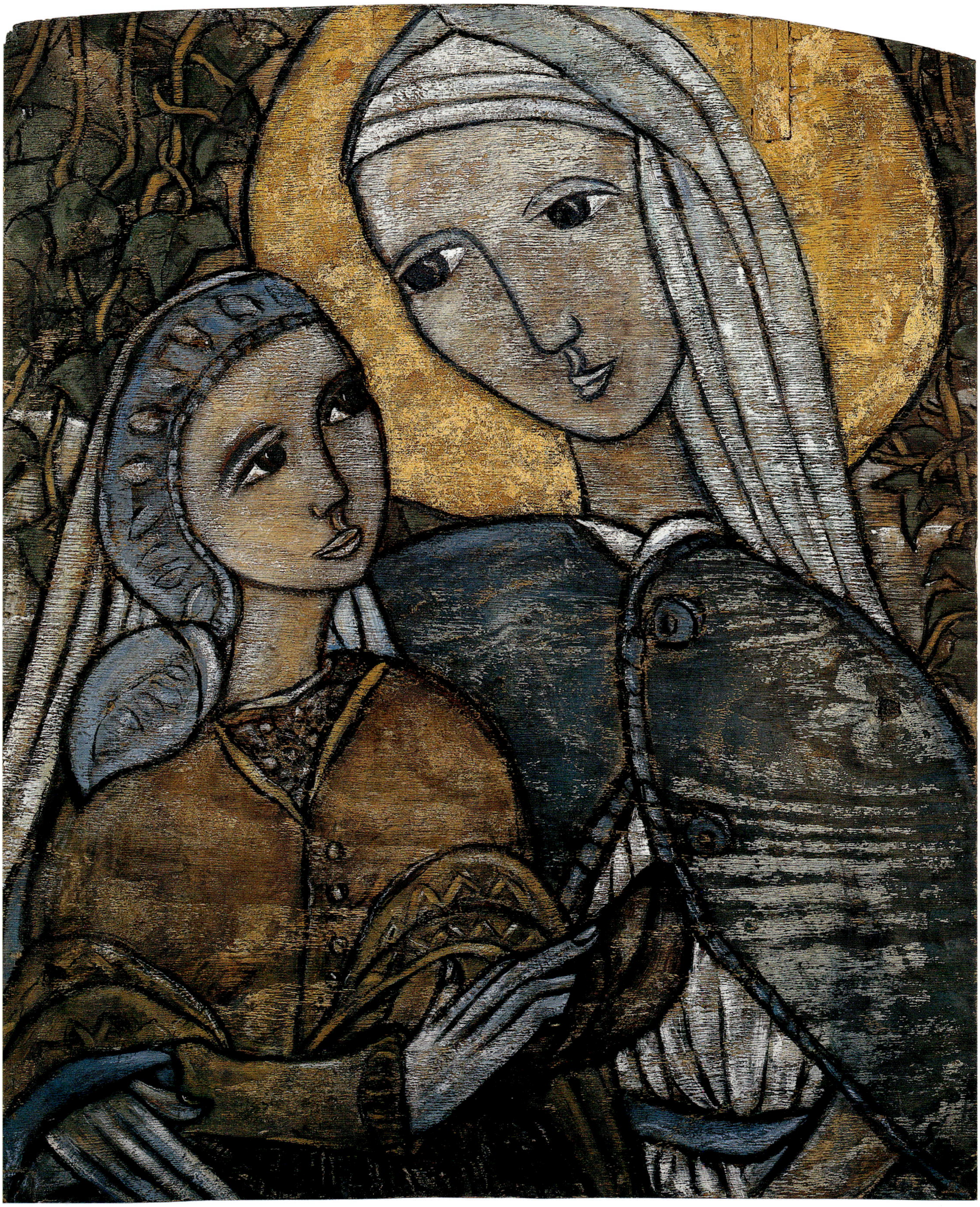

BERNADETTE MEETS PEYRAMALE

WORD *had quickly spread of Bernadette's visitations at Massabielle and hundreds of people were arriving daily to visit Lourdes. Bernadette soon faced the local authorities who tirelessly examined her or disbelieved her truth. On one occasion Bernadette went to the local priest, M. Peyramale with a message from the Lady. On entering the house the priest asked: "Well now, why do you want to see me?" Bernadette replied, "Monsieur le Curé, the Lady of the grotto has ordered me to tell the priests that she wishes to have a chapel at Massabielle."*

"What is this lady's name?"
"I don't know," replied Bernadette.
"You have not asked her?"
"Yes, but when I ask her, she smiles but does not reply."
"And you assert that she has instructed you to tell me that she wants a chapel at Massabielle?"
"Yes."

At such a categorical assertion the excitable M. Peyramale flared up. "Girl," he cried, "you are out of your mind! What! A lady who goes and perches on a rock! A lady you don't know! A lady who is perhaps as lunatic as you! This woman comes and tells you to invite us to have a chapel built for her at the grotto! And you accept such messages? And you imagine we are fools enough to listen to them? Look here girl, you are just a little joker." He continued, "I can't believe it is the Blessed Virgin who spoke to you. You just thought she did, that's all. I went to the rocks of Massabielle myself yesterday and I thought I heard something move. It must have been the same with you. You probably heard some bird that was hiding there and you imagined it was the Blessed Virgin who spoke to you." But she replied, "If it was a bird, it wouldn't have spoken."

14½ x 13¾ inches
Ink, gouache on paper

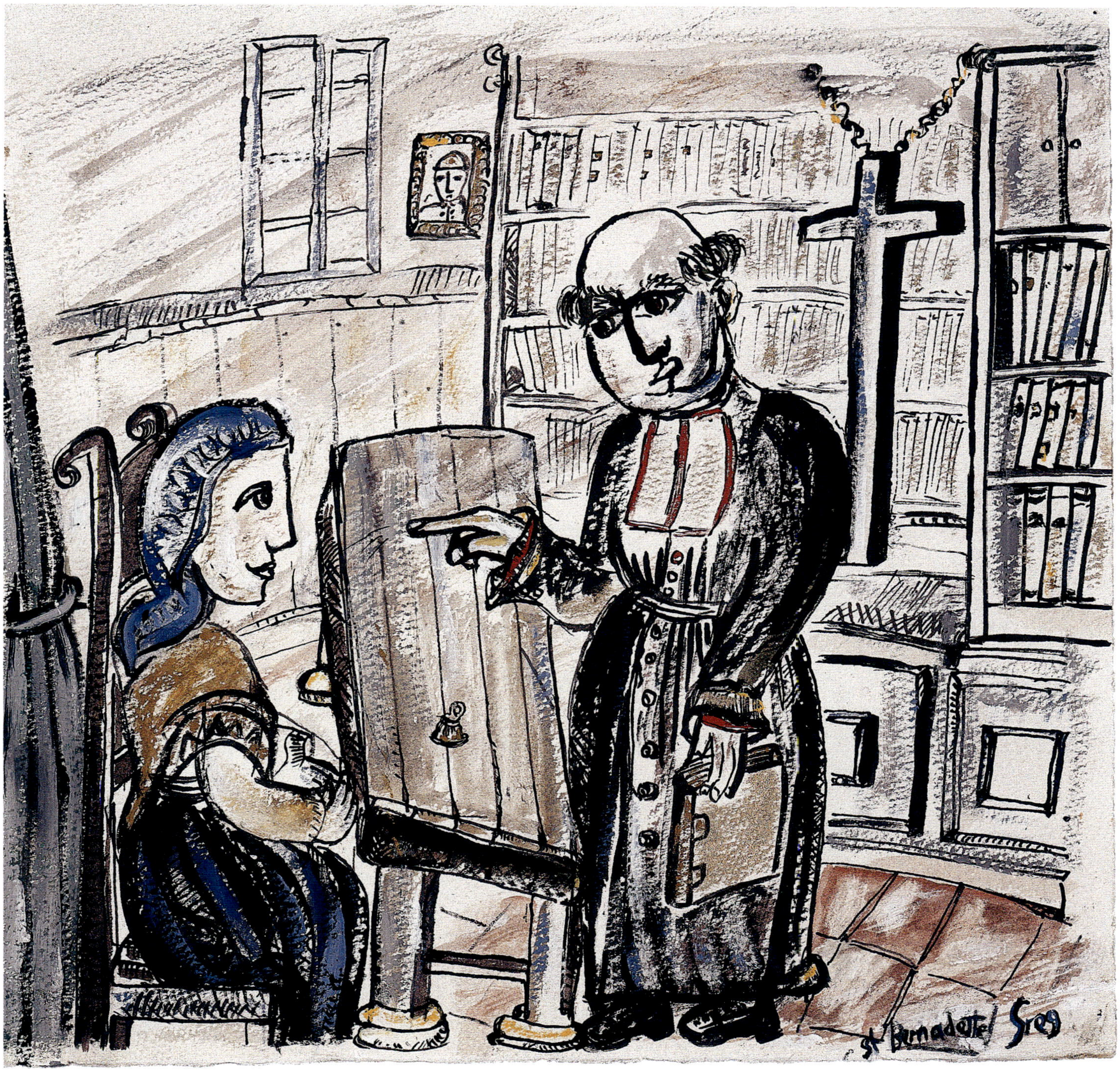
St Bernadette

GIRL WITH THE APPLE - LE CACHOT

AT *Le Cachot, with so many visitors coming to see Bernadette, she went to the room upstairs at her uncle André Sajous' to breathe more easily. Visitors walked down the dark hallway, through the small yard past the manure pile and climbed the open air staircase, which was pretty shaky.*

A girl of six years old whose arms and hands were partially paralysed came to see Bernadette. The paralysed child looked at Bernadette and then down at her apron pocket where a red apple was sticking out. The child's arms jerkily beat the air in the direction of the apple. Bernadette kindly responded and placed the apple in the hollow of the girl's hand with her bent fingers. The apple fell, rolling a number of times on the floor as her hands jerked each time, causing the apple to fall again. But when the girl left she managed a smile, feeling a little better. People would talk of a new miracle.

21¼ x 18¾ inches
Pastel, charcoal and oil on wood

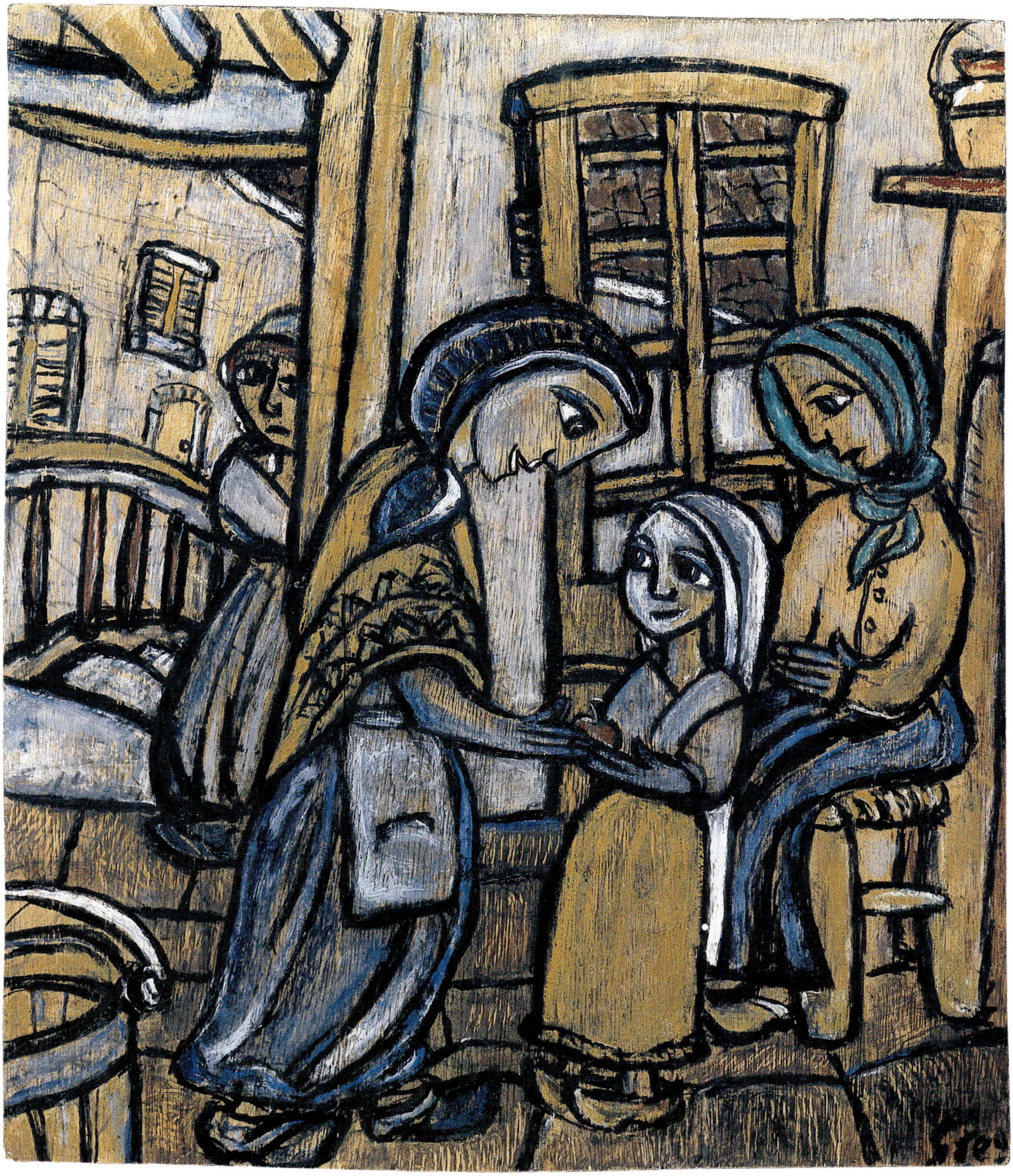
Frey

CHILDREN PLAYING AT LE CACHOT

11½ x 15¾ inches
Ink and watercolour on paper

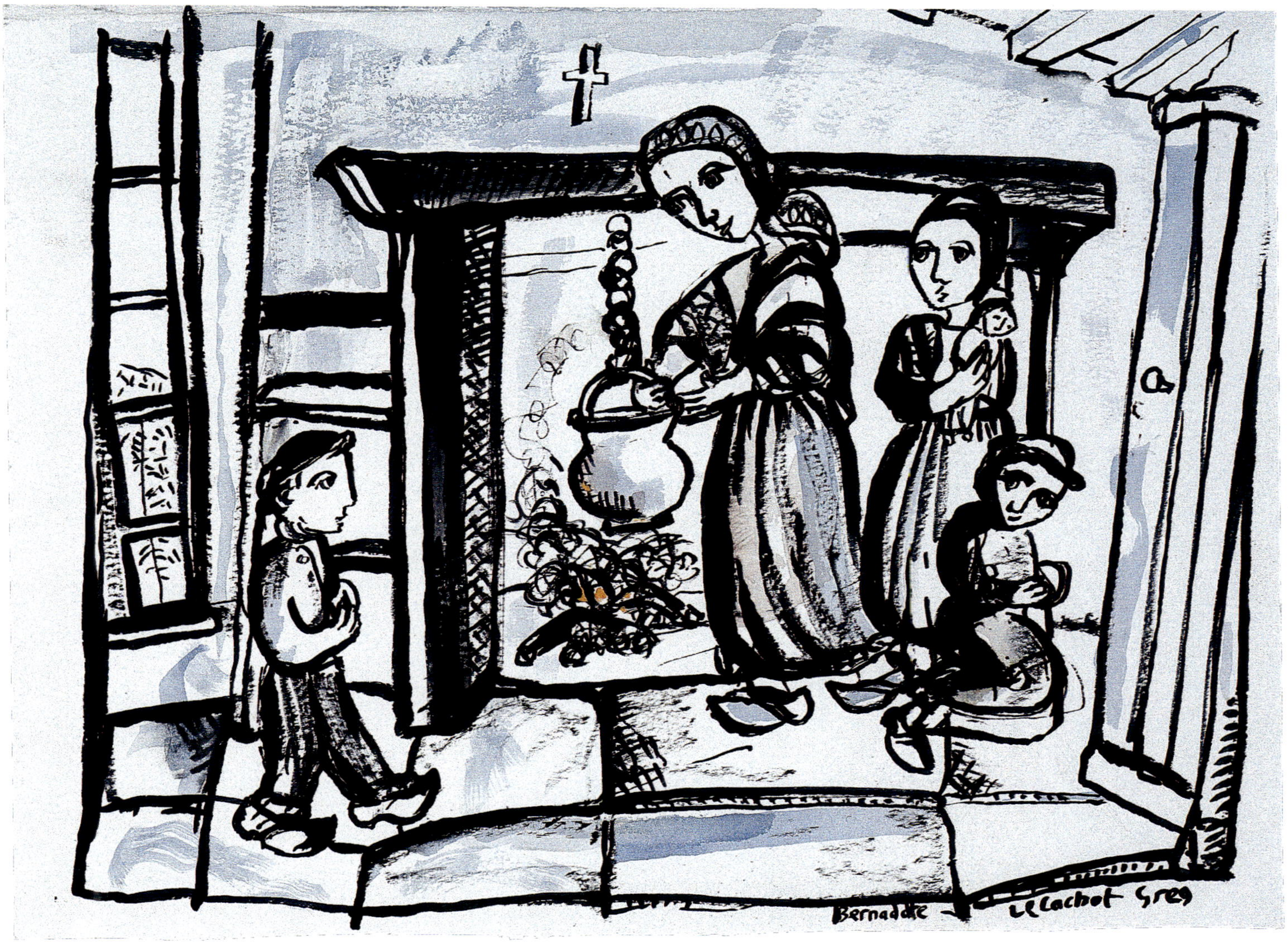
Bernadette
Le Cachot
Greg

BERNADETTE SKIPPING AT LOURDES HOSPICE

BERNADETTE *still attended the hospice sister school in Lourdes. She was full of fun, sometimes up to mischief, and on her way to school carried a shabby basket, at the bottom of which she had a stocking to knit, a crust of black bread, and her dog-eared spelling book. During break times in the hospice playground she merrily joined in the games with delightful abandon, laughing, singing and skipping with her friends. Bernadette would say that books were not meant for her and she had difficulty learning to read or write. She attended the school from June 1858 when she returned from Bartrès until she left for Nevers Convent in July 1886.*

20¼ x 13½ inches
Gouache and ink on paper

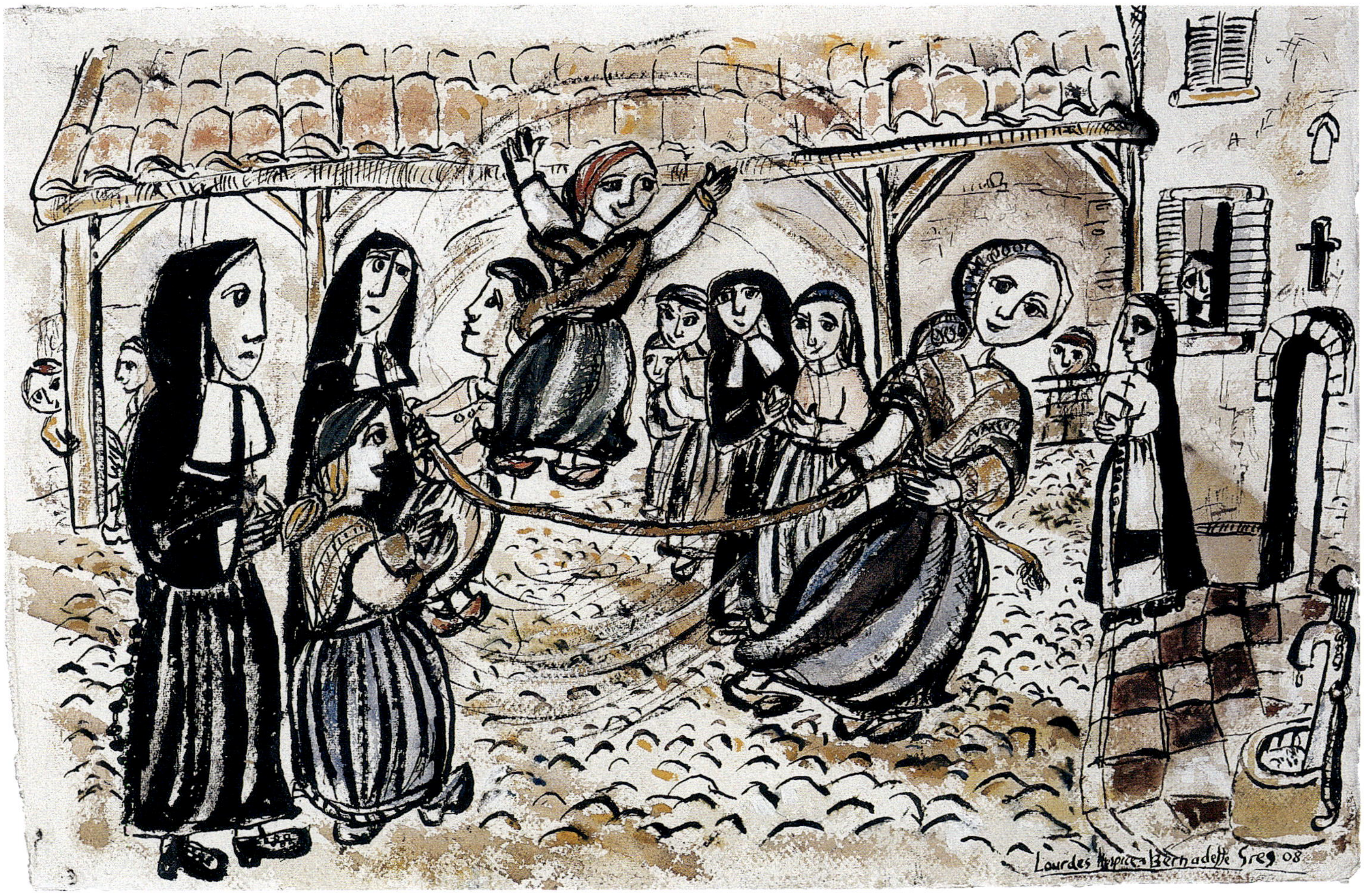
Lourdes Hospice Bernadette Greg 08

BERNADETTE AT THE WINDOW

HUNDREDS *of people would come to Bernadette's house and present their rosaries for her to touch. Bernadette would say: "I'll touch them with mine; take care of them not because I have touched them but because they have touched the beads I used during the apparitions." The crowds outside were clamouring to see Bernadette so she showed herself at the window. The gendarmes had a mounted guard over the Soubirous home, partly to keep order over the crowds, but secretly to make sure no money was being exchanged.*

15¼ x 11½ inches
Watercolour, ink and pencil on paper

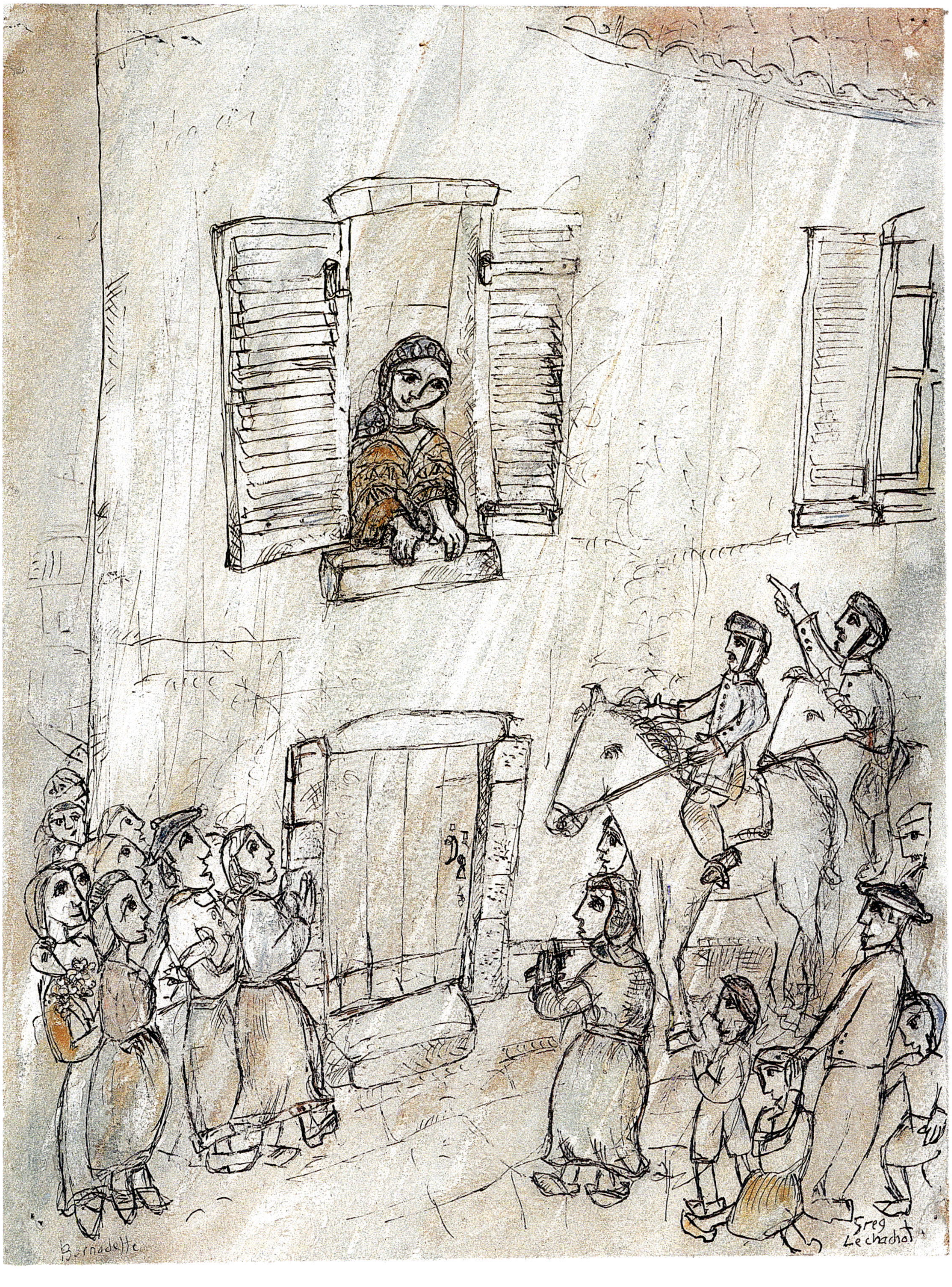
Bernadette
Greg
Lechachot

BERNADETTE ENTERS NEVERS CONVENT

BERNADETTE *took a few of her belongings with her when she left Lourdes. She had a rough canvas bag, a brolly and a trunk of linen that the sisters gave her. A large group of people waved goodbye as Bernadette left for Nevers, leaving her family and friends. She travelled by train, stopping at Bordeaux and Périgueux arriving at Nevers convent in the evening. The large convent gates closed. Bernadette now left forever her life as a shepherdess in Lourdes and the Pyrenees, and entered the silent and hidden world of the Sisters of Saint Gildard. She was given a short welcome by the Mother General and, as was the custom, taken to the statue of the Virgin at the Novitiate. From now on, Bernadette would be known as Marie-Bernarde.*

19¾ x 16 inches
Watercolour, gouache and ink on paper

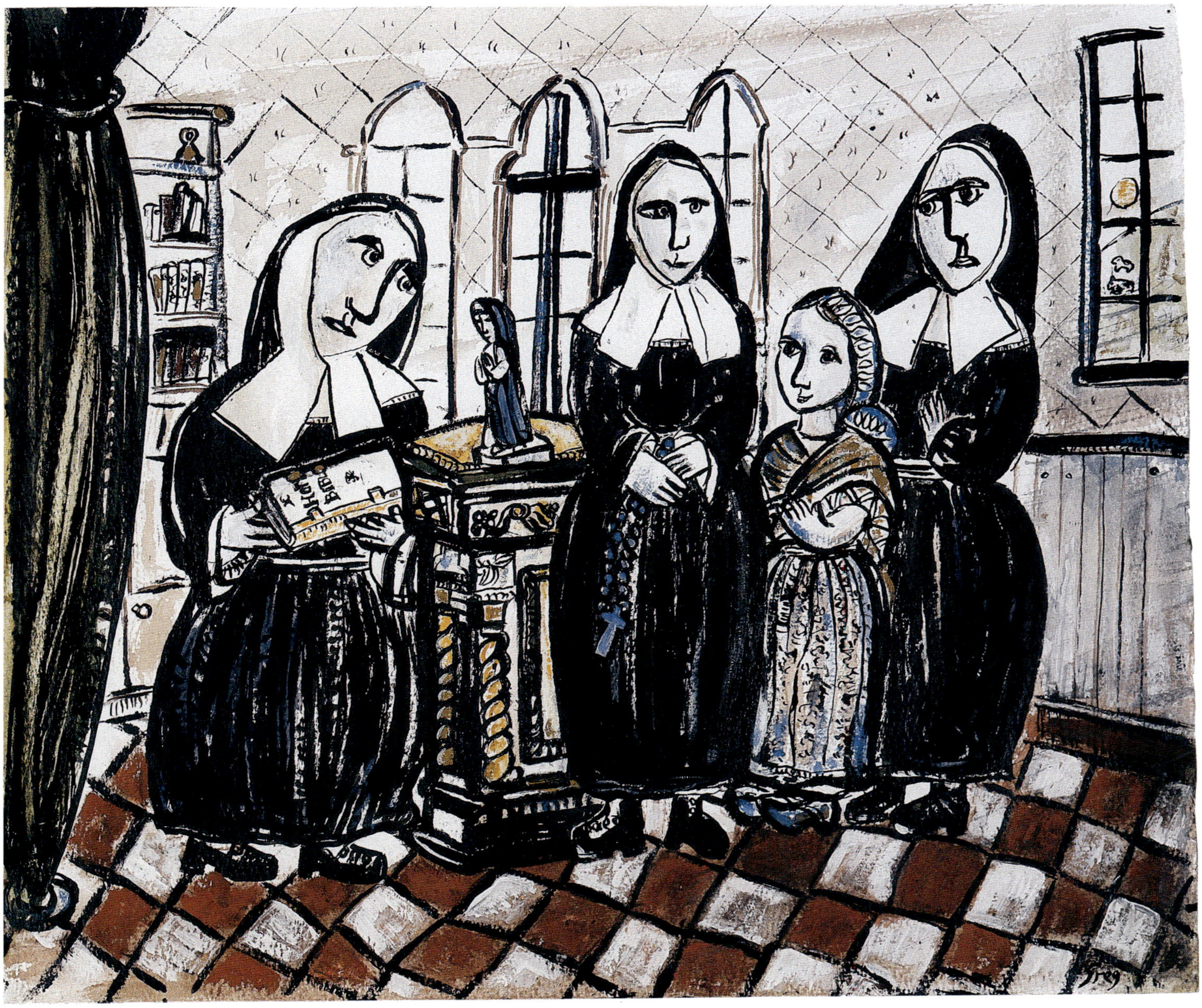

THE BUNCH OF GRAPES

AFTER *the grape harvest in October 1877, the community went to Saint Joseph's chapel as was the custom to recite a short daily prayer. While walking past a big wall facing the chapel, Bernadette suddenly noticed a large bunch of grapes left hanging just above the latticed water tank that irrigated the garden. "What a shame to let such beautiful grapes go to waste," said Bernadette. "If we tried to get them we could enjoy them."*

No sooner was this said, than the other sisters helped form a stepladder by crisscrossing their hands. Bernadette took off her shoes and climbed up to reach the golden cluster of grapes. After climbing down she dashed off to the Venerable Mother of Nevers who was walking ahead and asked her permission to divide them; which she did.

14 x 15½ inches
Gouache, ink and watercolour on paper

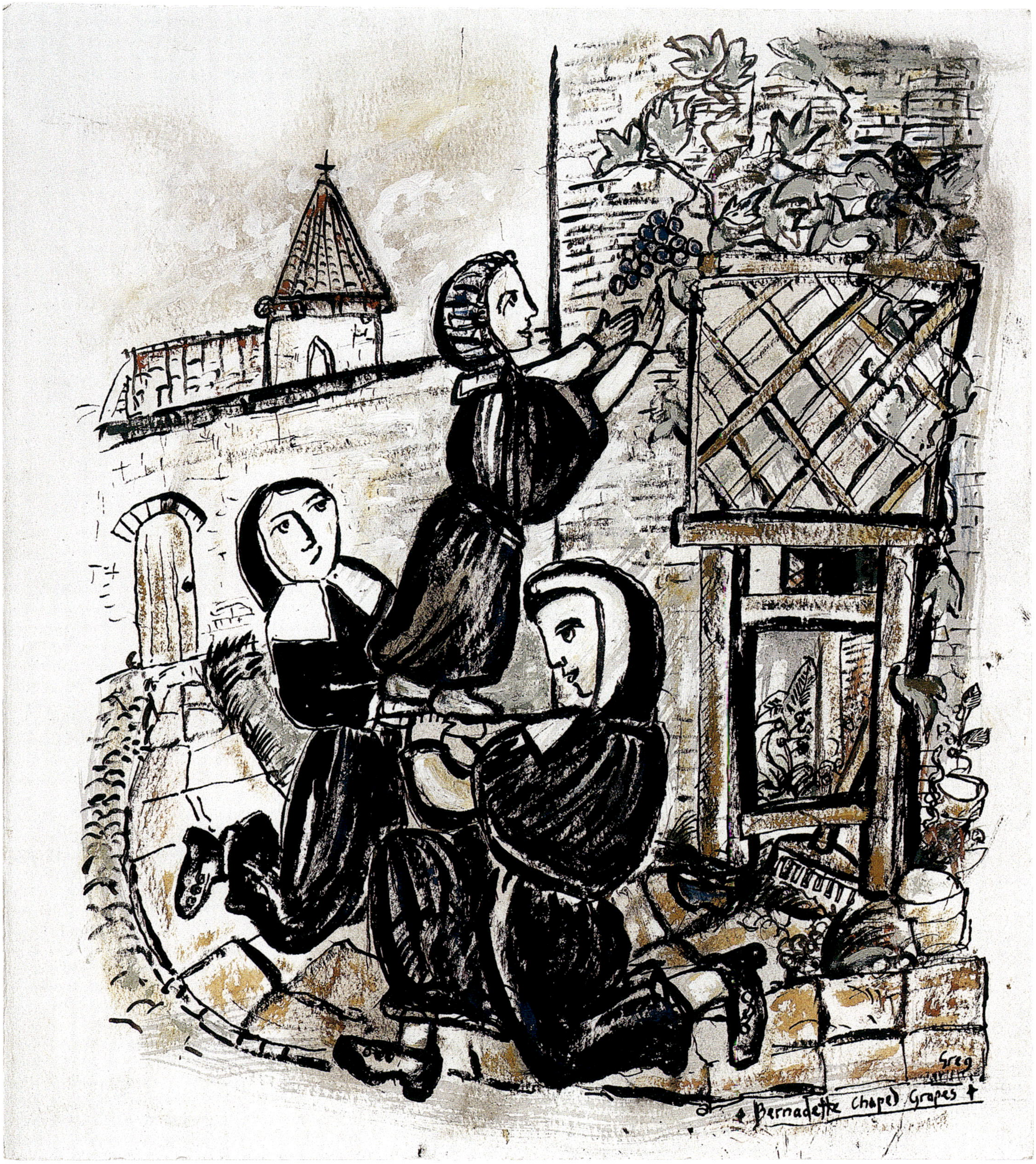
Greg
Bernadette Chapel Grapes

ROLLING CARROTS

ONE DAY *when Bernadette was on refectory duty, she sat down at the table after most of the sisters had gone. That day there was a platter of carrots sliced into thin circles. They were hard and Bernadette picked at the plate with the fork, sending the carrots rolling down the table. It was impossible not to laugh. Bernadette was laughing so hard that the other sisters did too. They couldn't eat anymore after that.*

22 x 16 inches
Oil on canvas

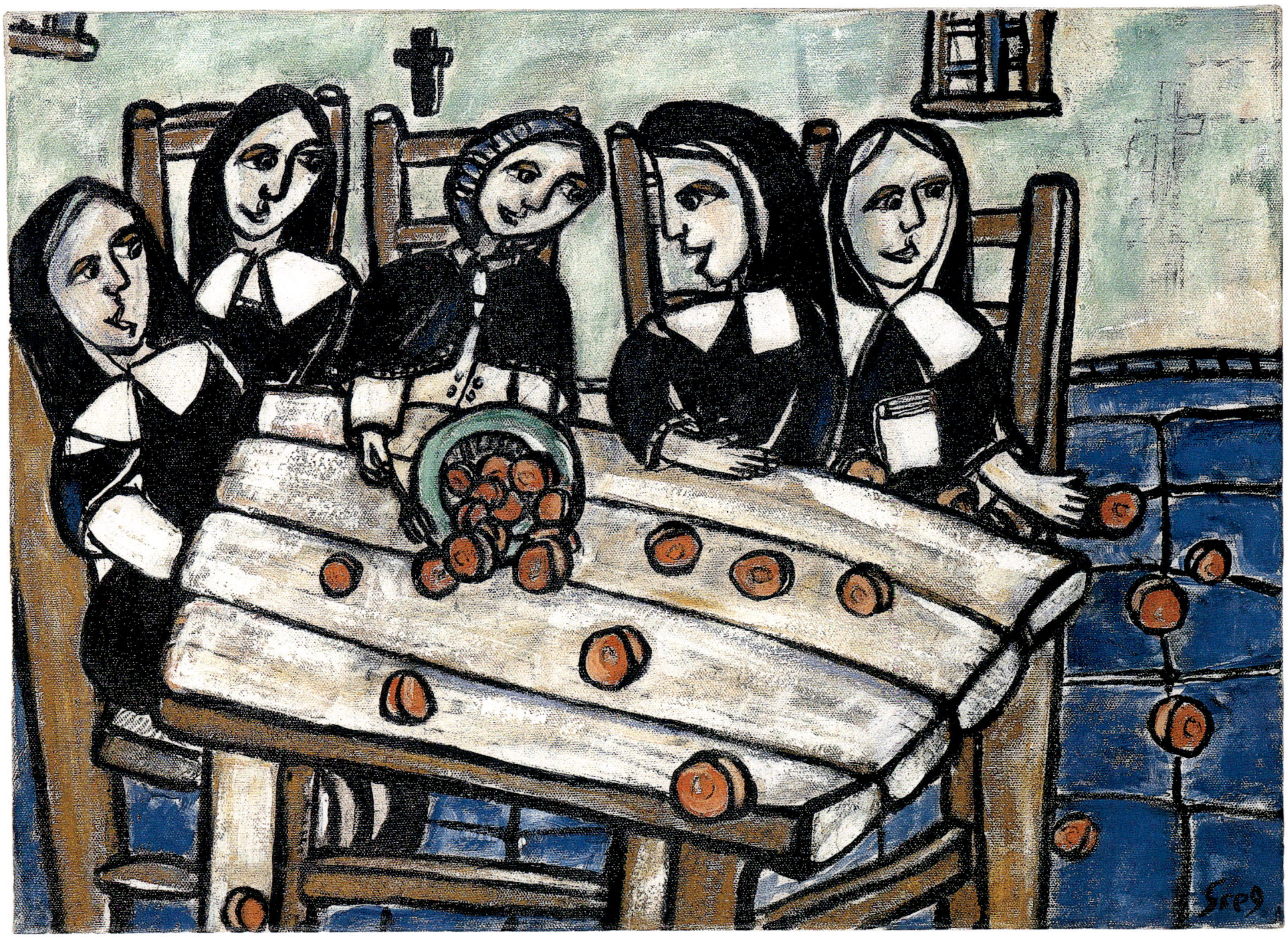

VISIT TO VARENNES ORPHANAGE

IN *January 1873 Bernadette suffered an acute attack of asthma, but towards Easter she managed to recover a little. After a precarious convalescence, on May 12th Mother Joséphine Imbert took advantage of the fine weather to visit the Varennes Orphanage with Bernadette by coach. They also visited the school at Coulanges-lès-Nevers, a large village three kilometres from Nevers on the banks of the Nieve. Bernadette was particularly fond of this lovely stretch of river and trees. When the bell announced their arrival, the many children would rush out from the workrooms, classrooms, kitchens, wash-houses and gardens to greet them.*

19½ x16 inches
Ink and gouache on paper

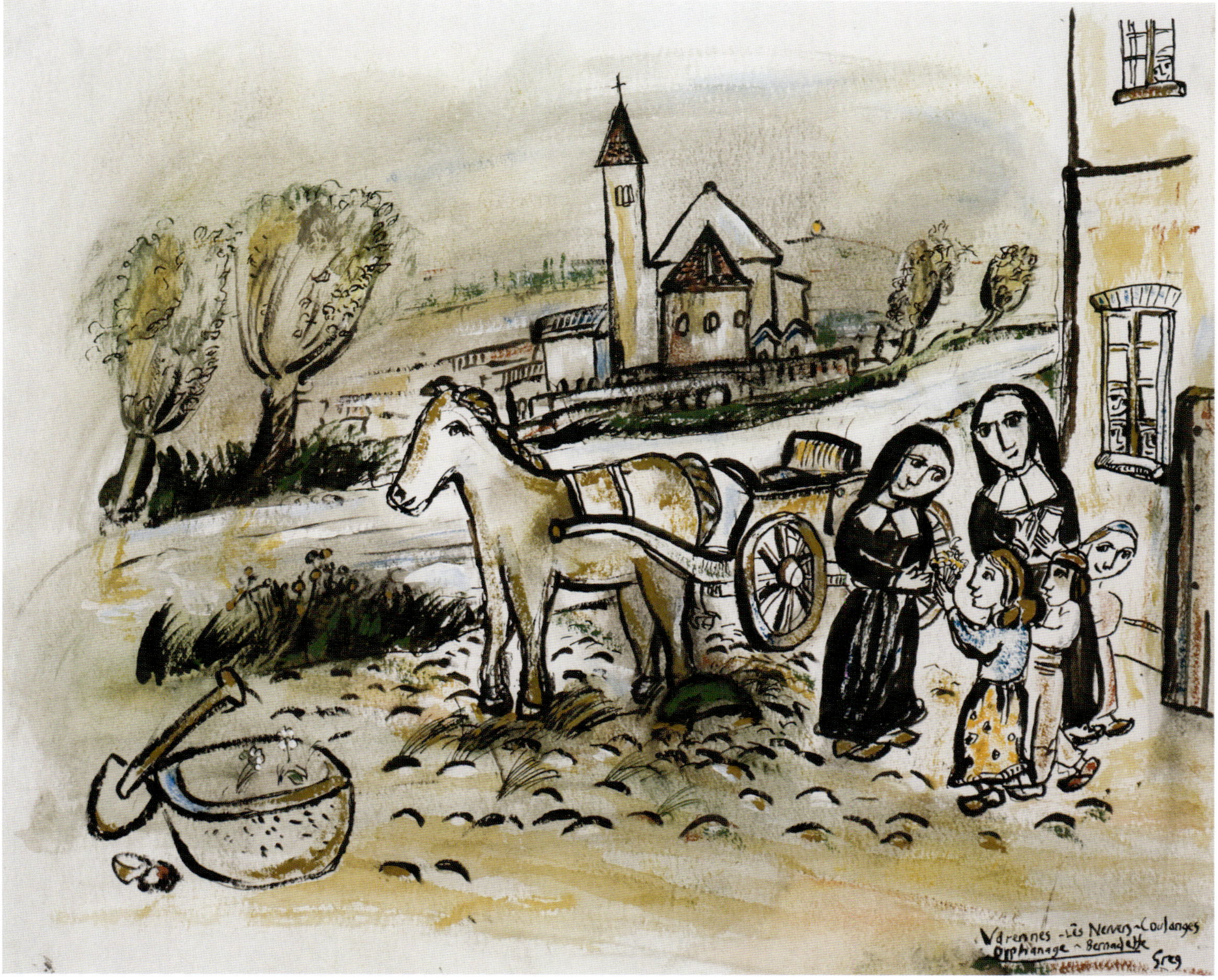
Varennes - Lès Nevers - Coulanges
Orphanage - Bernadette
Greg

BERNADETTE WITH FLOWERS

DURING *her novitiate at Nevers Bernadette had, for a while, been assistant Sacristan. She loved her work and took delight in decorating Our Lady's altar. The work for her was no mere matter of routine or habit. As she performed her duties near the altar she was filled with the thought of God's presence, showing always great reverence and deep regard for holy things.*

14 x 11½ inches
Gouache, ink and watercolour on paper

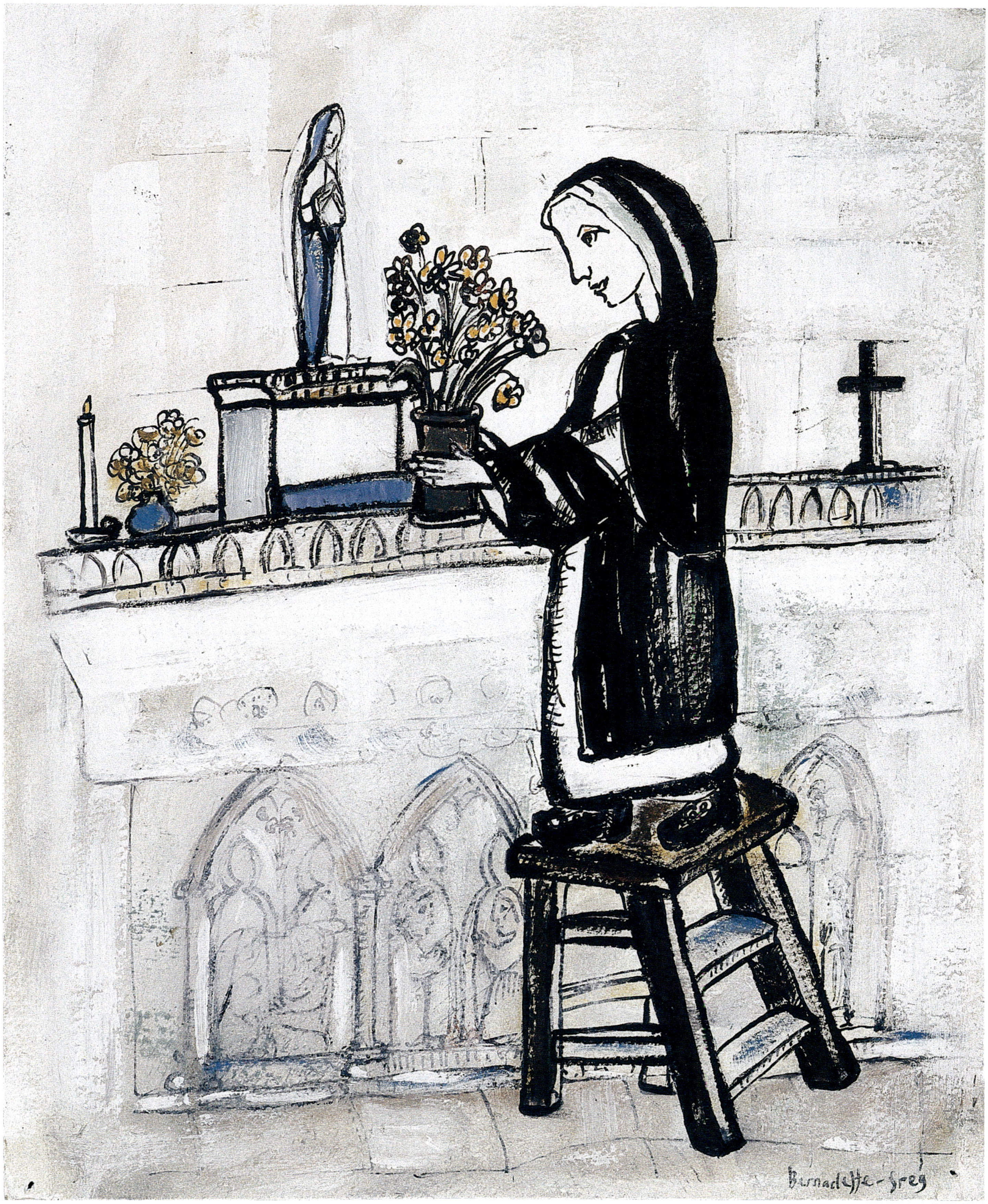

BERNADETTE'S EMBROIDERY

IN FINE WEATHER *Bernadette took her embroidery work into the corner of the cloister where she was sheltered from the wind. There she spent long hours in solitude and silence. Growing frail now during her last days on her path: on the way of the cross, Bernadette experienced a deeper union with the Christ.*

25 x 20½ inches
Charcoal and acrylic on hessian

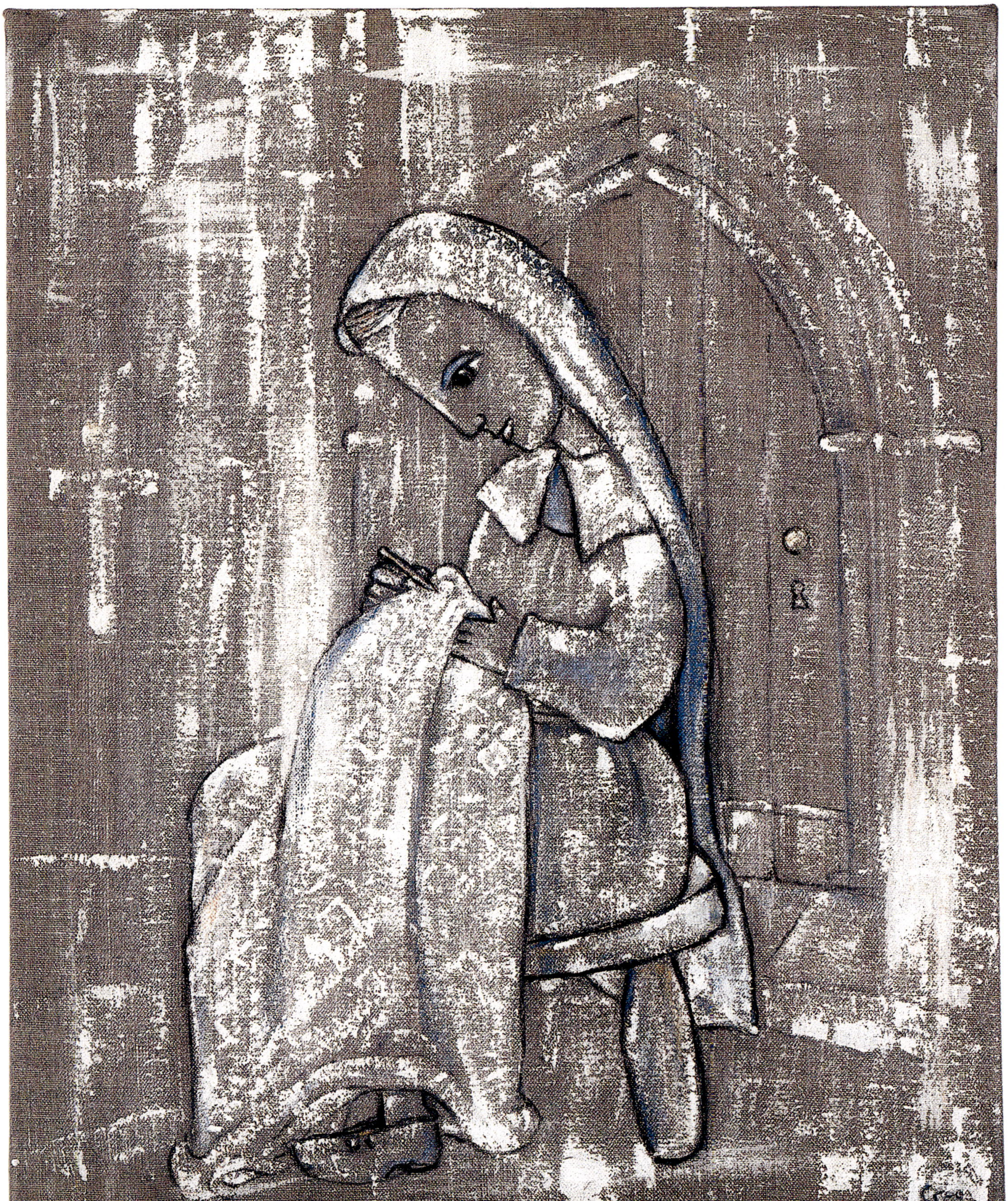

THE WHITE CHAPEL

"I'm being ground like a grain of wheat."

Bernadette.

Bernadette died at Nevers Convent, Easter 1879

23¼ x 24¼ inches
Oil on wood

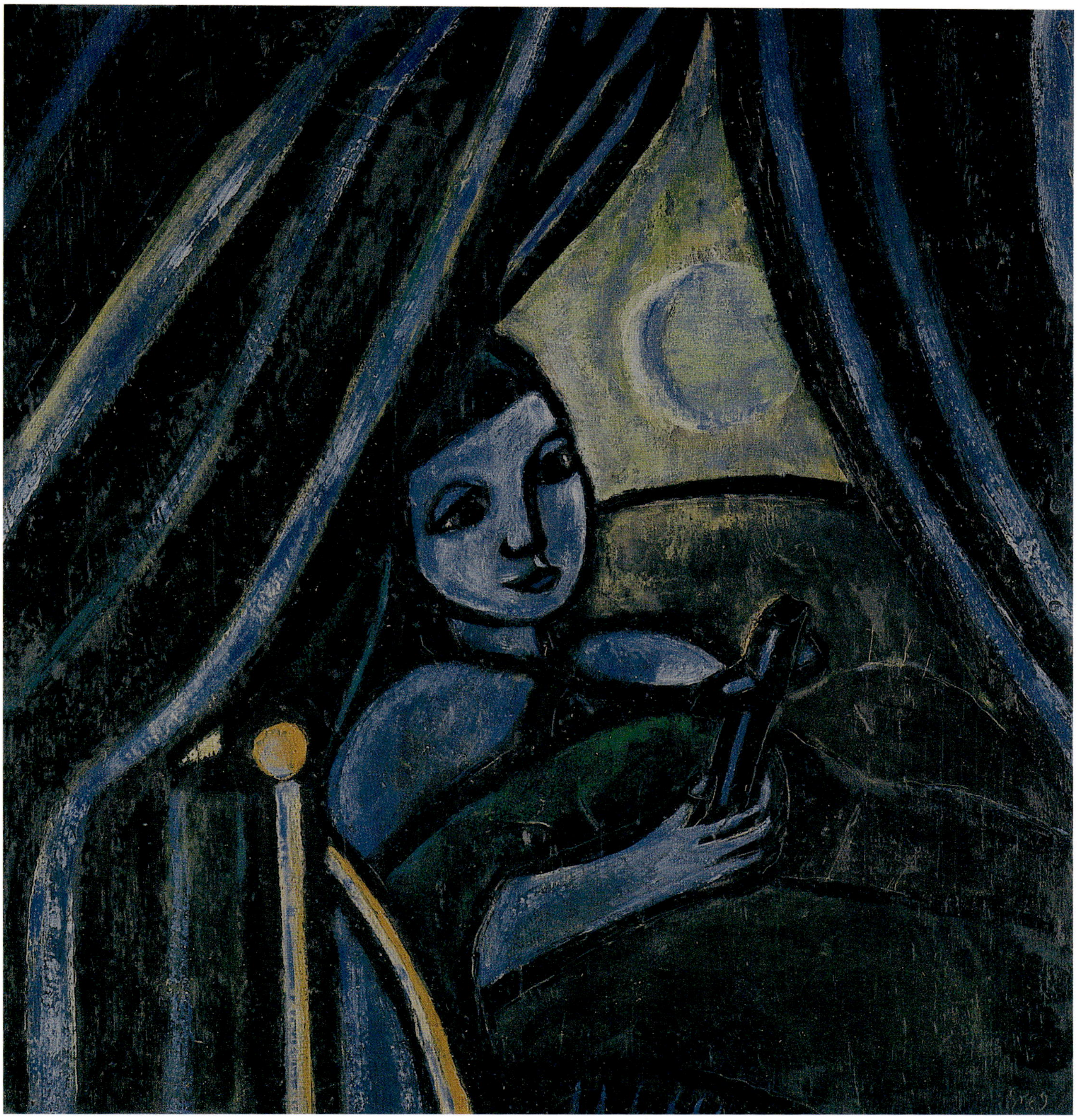

ICON - ST BERNADETTE - THE DOOR

48 x 42 inches
Oil and gold leaf on wood door

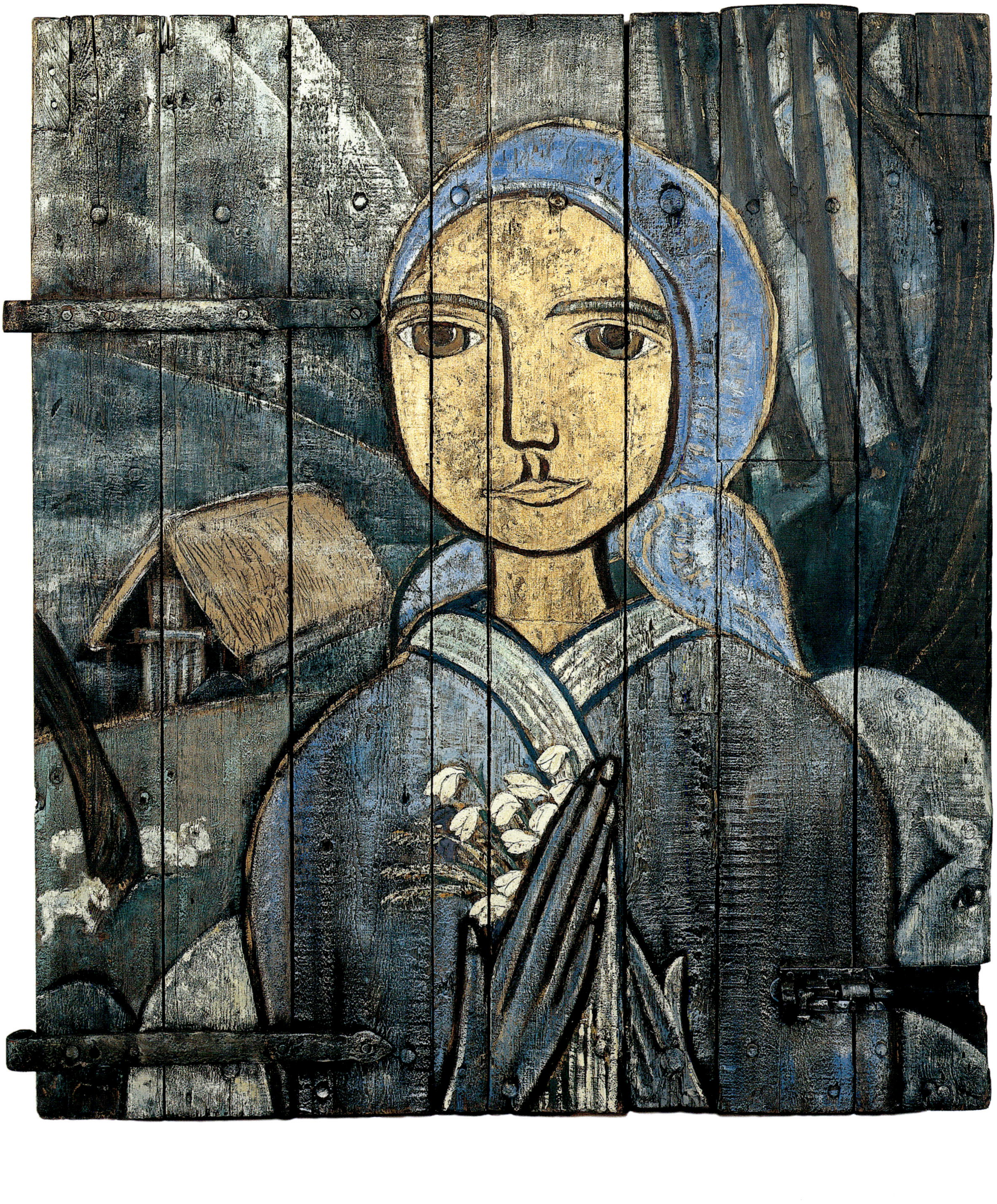

Bibliography

During his researches, Philip Vann found two books on Bernadette especially illuminating, and has gratefully quoted from them in his essay:

Bernadette and Lourdes, Michel de Saint-Pierre, Translated by Edward Fitzgerald, Hutchinson & Co., London, 1954

Bernadette of Lourdes: A Life Based on Authenticated Documents, René Laurentin, translated by John Drury, Darton, Longman & Todd, London, 1979

In researching the life of Bernadette, Greg Tricker has found the following books inspiring and helpful:

Bernadette of Lourdes, Frances Parkinson Keyes, Hollis & Carter, London, 1955

Saint Bernadette Soubirous, Abbé François Trochu, Longmans Press, London, 1957

Bernadette Speaks: A Life of Saint Bernadette Soubirous in Her Own Words, René Laurentin, Pauline Books and Media, Boston, MA, 1999

Lourdes: Body and Spirit in the Secular Age, Ruth Harris, Penguin Books, London, 1999

Isis Mary Sophia: Her Mission and Ours, Rudolf Steiner, Rudolf Steiner Books, London, 2003

The Golden Age of Chartres, René M.Querido, Floris Books, ISBN 0-86315-058-6

APPENDIX

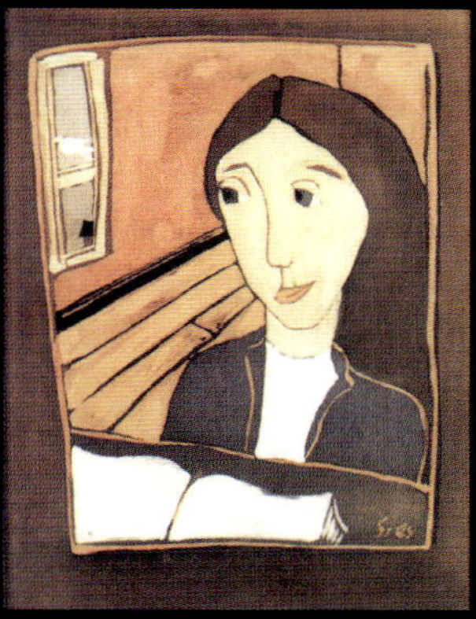
1

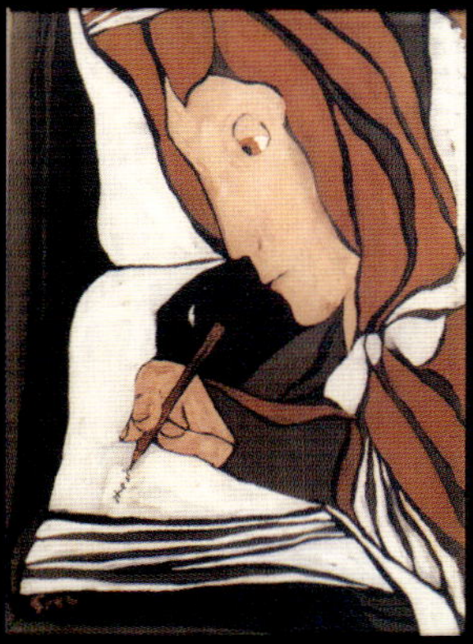
2

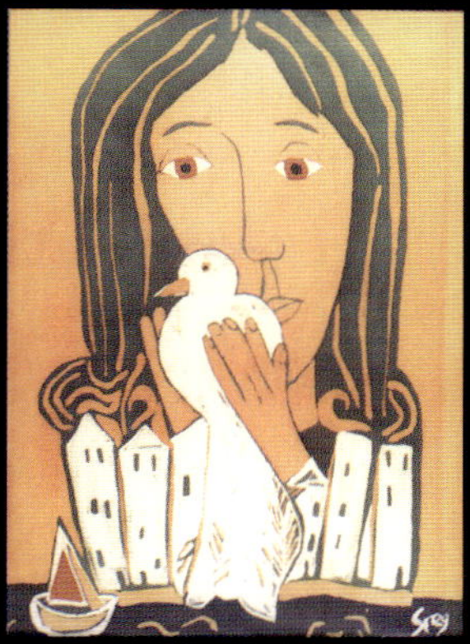
3

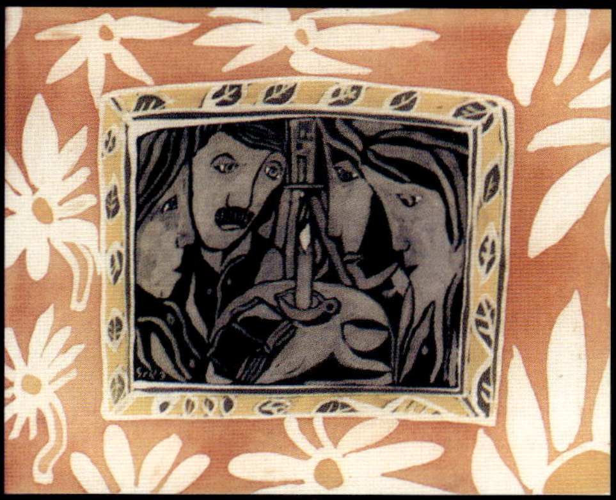
4

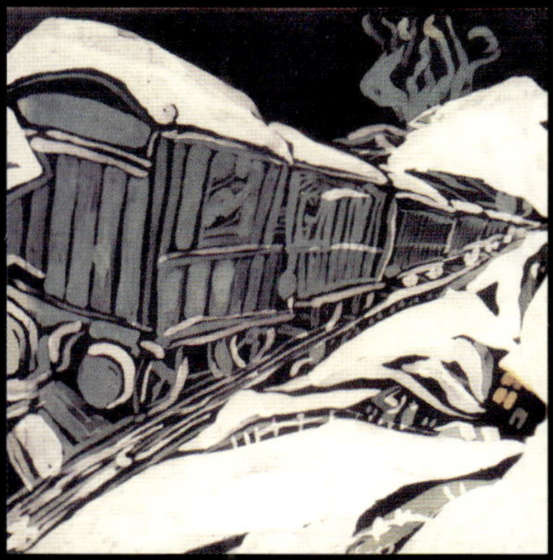
5

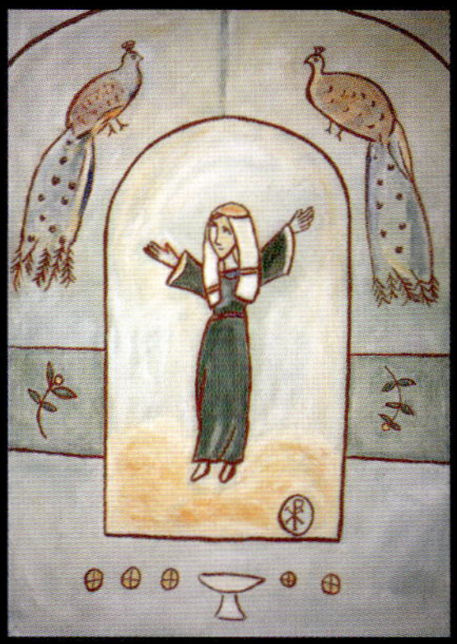
6

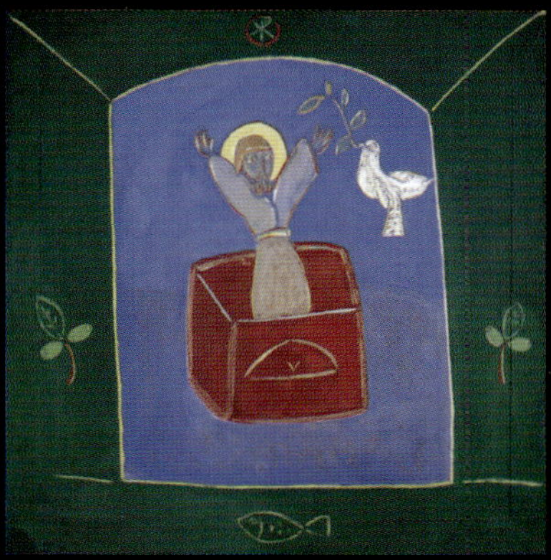
7

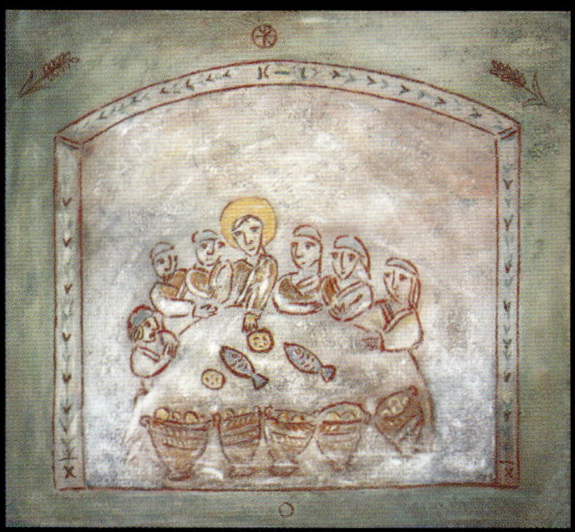
8

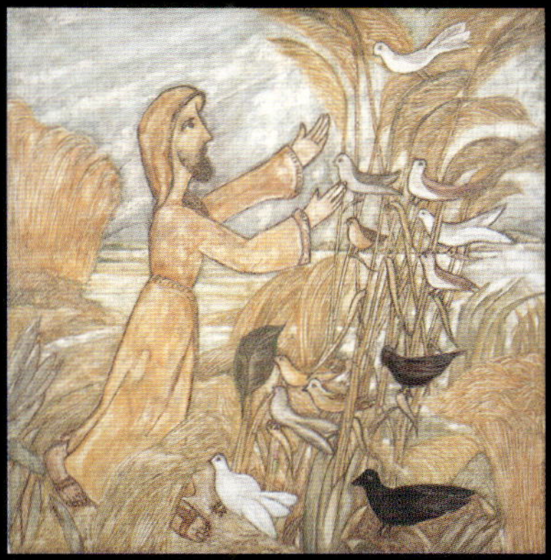
9

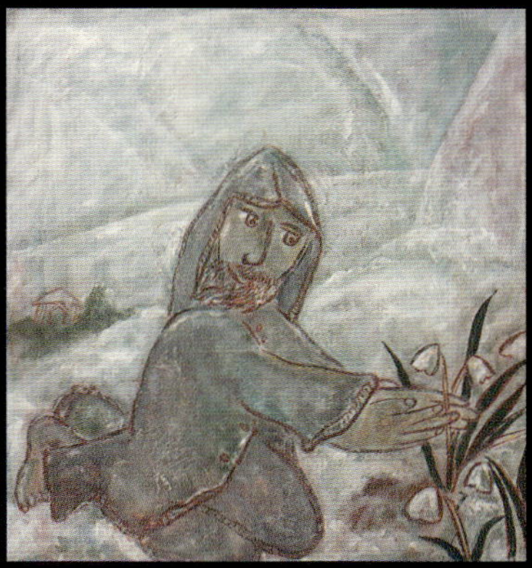
10

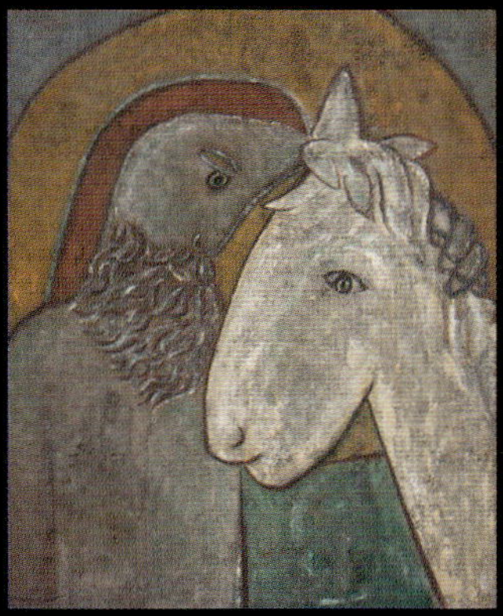
11

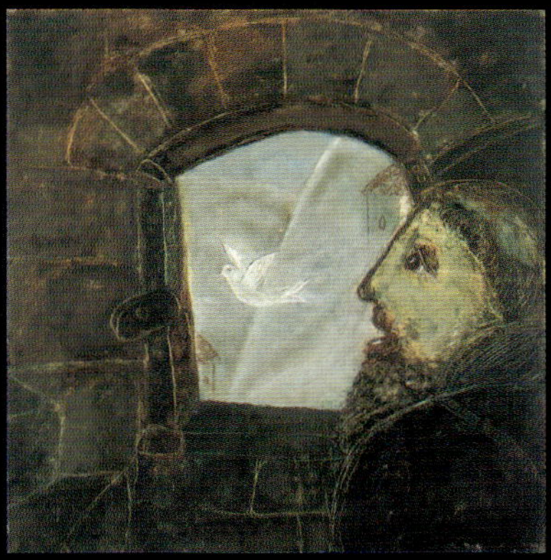
12

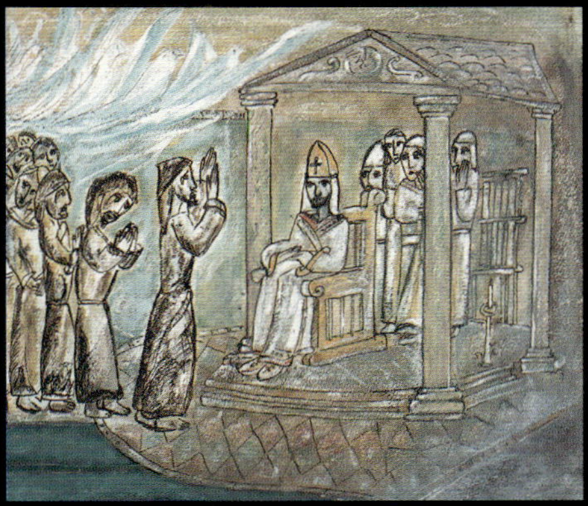
13

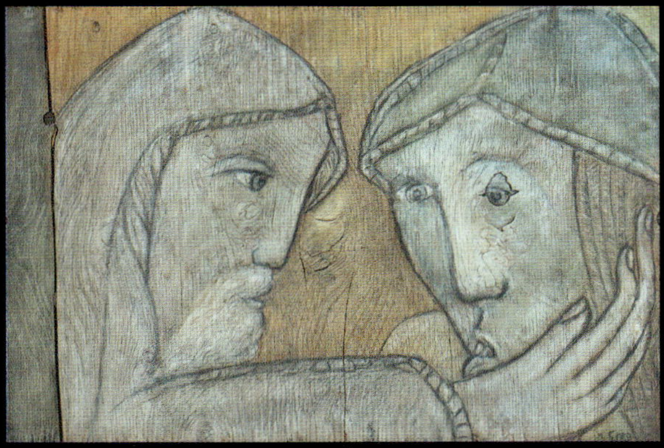
14

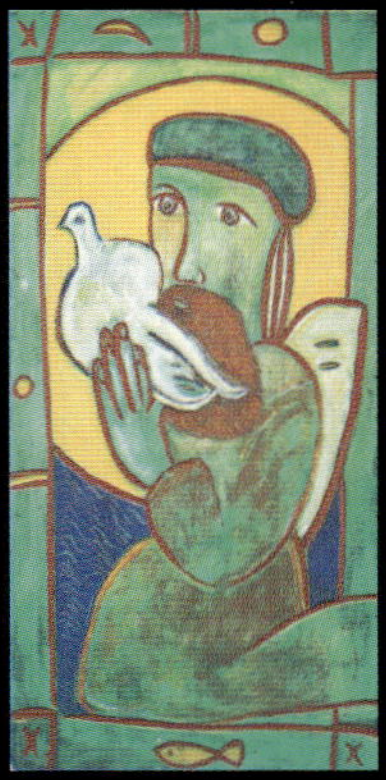
15

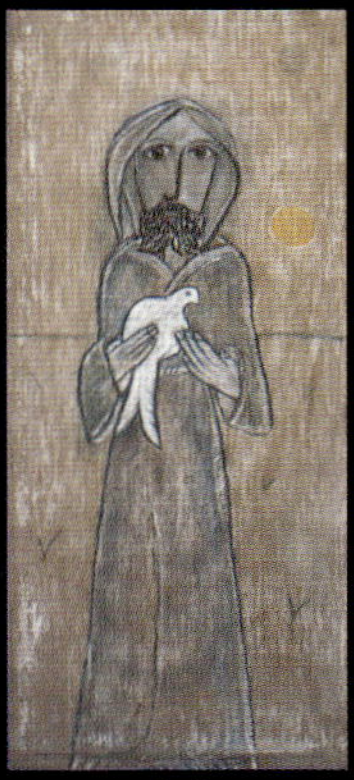
16

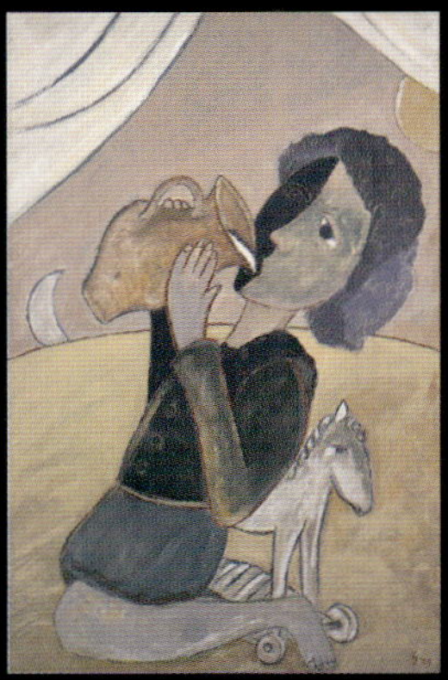
17

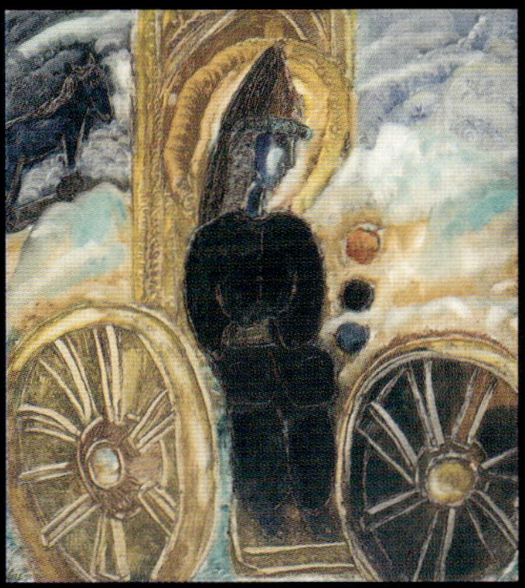
18

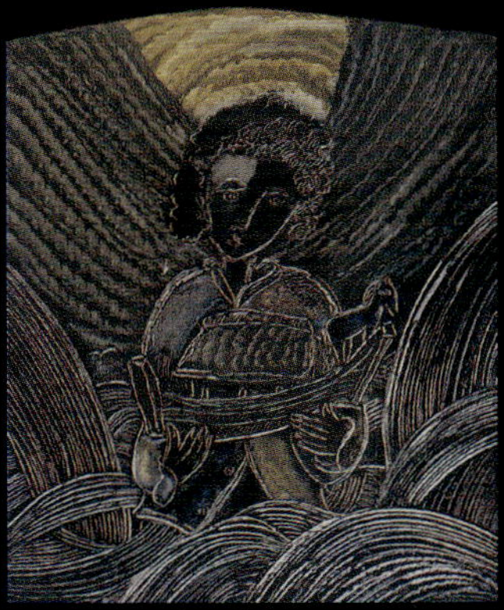
19

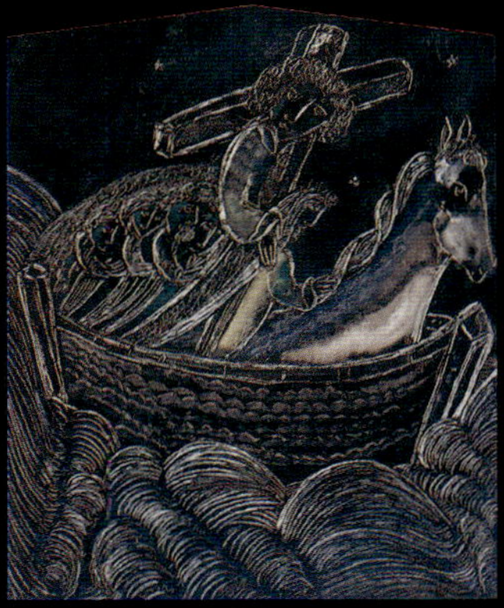
20

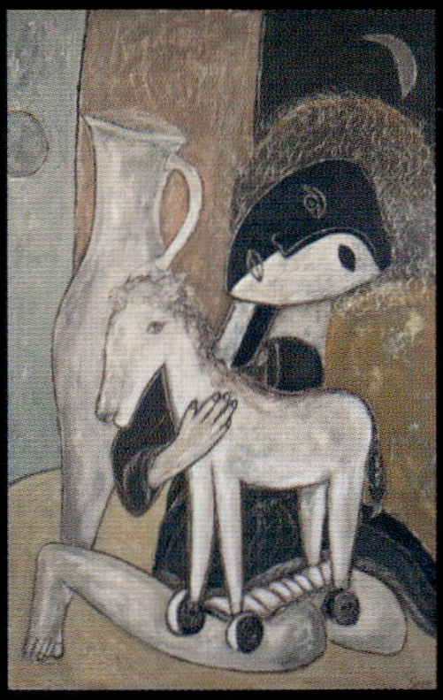
21

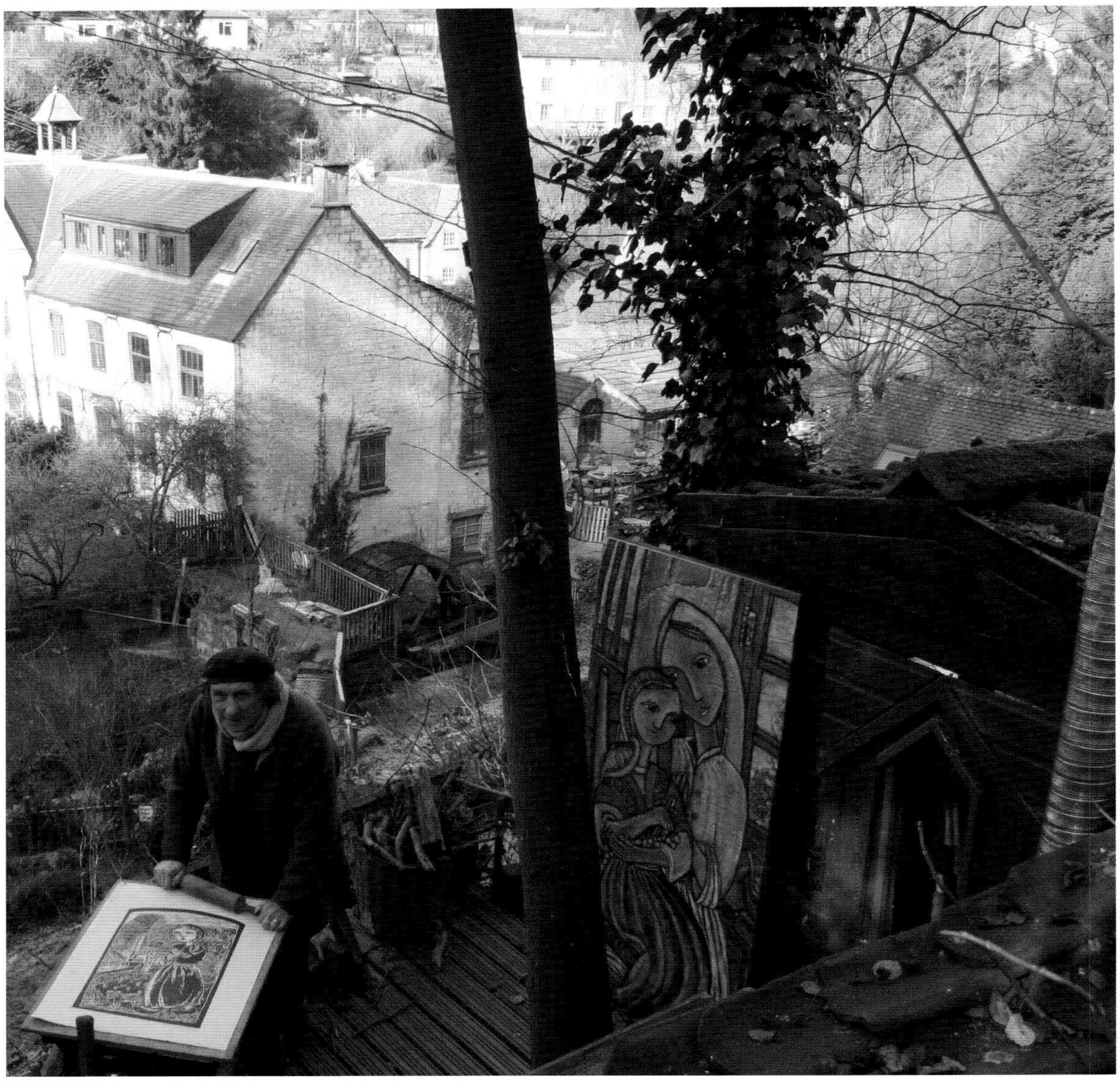

Photo by Francis Naydler

Greg Tricker's Studio at Millbottom in Nailsworth

Other Books by Greg Tricker

Francis of Assisi - Paintings For Our Time
Paintings by Greg Tricker, Text by Johannes Steuck
Green Books; Tel: 01803 863260
Gloucestershire, 2005
ISBN 903998-66-2
Format 330 x 221mm x 60 colour plates
Hard Bound
Price £25.00

This inspired collection of over sixty original paintings, stone carvings and woodcut prints by Greg Tricker portrays the human suffering, exultation, compassion and joy of the life of St Francis; with their visionary quality, they present a fresh, contemporary image of St Francis.

Kaspar Hauser - The Holy Fool & The Path of Sacrifice
Paintings by Greg Tricker; Text by Johannes Steuck, Forward by Jonathan Stedall
Wynstones Press, Tel: 01384 399455
Gloucestershire, 2006
ISBN 0-9542873-1-2
Hard Bound
Price £25.00

The following books are available from Greg Tricker at:
The Cottage, Millbottom, Nailsworth GLOS GL6 0LA
Tel: 01453 834975

The Catacombs
Paintings by Greg Tricker, Text by Johannes Steuck
21 Colour Plates; Format 250 x 290mm
Gloucestershire, 2002
Price £17.50

The paintings and stone carvings are centred around early Christianity and are inspired by the wall paintings in the catacombs, the ancient burial chambers found beneath Rome dating from 1st-3rd century AD

For Anne Frank
21 Colour Plates; Format 215 x 150mm
With poems by Nick Naydler
Bristol, 1991
Price £7.00

For Alice Rose
11 Colour Etchings and 10 Line Drawings
With Poems by Nick Naydler
£8.50 + p&p